MOORISH STYLE

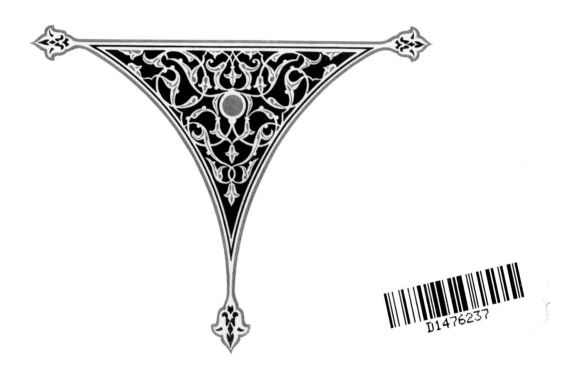

MOORISH STYLE

MILES DANBY

Φ

Endpapers: Detail of a carved ivory panel from an early eleventh-century casket.

Half-title page: An ornamental pattern from the spandrel beneath the dome of the Suleimaniye Mosque in Istanbul. This illustration is Plate 37 from *The Grammar of Ornament* (1856) by Owen Jones.

Half-title verso: An interior at the Alhambra in a coloured lithograph (1853) by Baron Isidore Taylor.

Title page: The design of this section of paving in the Alhambra incorporates a pomegranate. 'Granada' is the Spanish for pomegranate and it has been adopted as the city's symbol, although some scholars believe the name has a Moorish origin.

Page 5: A semicircular arch at the Alhambra with two windows set with perforated screens beneath.

Phaidon Press Limited

Regent's Wharf

All Saints Street

London N1 9PA

First published 1995
Reprinted in paperback 1999
© 1995 Phaidon Press Limited

A CIP catalogue record for this book is available from the British Library

ISBN 0 7148 3861 6

Printed in Hong Kong

CONTENTS

Opposite: Although enti-
tled *The Moorish Bath*,
(c.1870), this painting by
the French painter Jean-
Léon Gérôme actually
depicts an Egyptian scene,
the result of Gérôme's
visit to Cairo in 1868. Such
scenes of sensual delight
were intended to appeal
to rich male collectors.

Right: This flowing monogram, or *tugra*, of Sultan
Ahmet is dated 1623. It
is a brilliant calligraphic
composition of vertical
strokes and horizontal
loops and forms part of
an official document
recording the charitable
gifts of Gevher Sultan.

Spain is half African, Africa is half Asian.
Victor Hugo

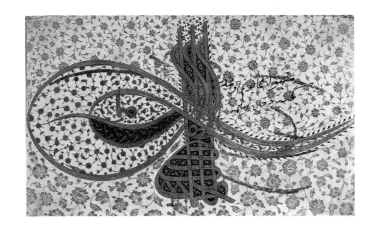

The past has always held an attraction for those distracted by or recoiling from the discomforts of the present. Written records and images of past events have provided fertile ground for the imagination. Never was nostalgia for the past greater than in Northern Europe at the beginning of the nineteenth century; as expanding industrialization was creating a bleak, inhuman environment so Romantic literature increasingly turned to fantastic accounts of episodes in history. In architecture, design and decoration, the revival of historical styles was already fashionable but these were usually derived from what was perceived to be European culture. When it was possible to add an element of unfamiliarity, especially if it were warm and colourful, the attraction of the past became more powerful. The exotic past of the countries to the south and east of Europe was becoming more widely known as descriptions of historic buildings were published by travellers and miniature paintings from Persia and India found their way to the West. The latter depicted scenes of luxury and tranquillity, often showing social gatherings in gardens of exquisite beauty containing fountains and pavilions of intricate design. The figures were dressed in rich and elaborate costumes.

Climate also had a part to play in the Western fascination with the exotic. The contrast between the cold, grey, noisy and polluted environment of European cities and the warm, colourful image of the peaceful Persian garden inversely parallels the yearning of a Bedouin nomad in the harsh, burning desert for the cool, green comfort of the oasis and the soothing murmur of the fountain. Until modern times, such a dramatic change of environment was beyond the means of most. Besides pilgrims, whose faith enabled them to endure the discomforts and deprivations of travel, and apart from a relatively small number of writers and artists, only the wealthy could afford to travel to those distant lands where the unfamiliar could be experienced at first-hand. The less wealthy could let their imagination be carried by prose or poetry. A few affluent intellectuals, inspired by literature and painting, were able to create for themselves decorated spaces in a luxurious style that cannot easily be defined. Some prominent figures, like Sir Robert Shirley as early as 1609, indulged in having their portraits painted in Turkish or Eastern dress.

This view from within the Pearl Mosque (Moti Masjid) at Agra shows the entrance gateway and courtyard. It is one of a collection of photographs published in 1928 under the title *Picturesque India*. The mosque, which was built in 1648–55, is composed mainly of translucent polished marble; hence the title 'Pearl'. Even though it was built within the palace of the Red Fort, it was designed to accommodate a large congregation.

Depicting an idyllic scene in a beautiful garden, this 1565 Mogul miniature shows the Persian hero Rustum, attended by his servants, enjoying refreshments with his mistress, Mihr Afruz. The open octagonal kiosk in which they sit is placed in a court paved with blue ceramic tiles. This illustration is taken from *The Romance of Amir Hamza*.

Opposite: The celebrated French author and traveller Pierre Loti, dressed as a sultan, relaxes on a sofa in the Turkish room of his house at Rochefort. The house is now a museum displaying Loti's eclectic collection of treasures acquired on his journeys in the Middle East, Turkey, Africa, India and Oceania. These artefacts were the inspiration behind Loti's many late nineteenth-century novels. He also constructed a mosque lined with tiles brought back from Damascus.

Right: This tinted litho-graph by Louis Haghe after David Roberts, shows a street scene in the Beze-stein bazaar, Khan El Khalil, Cairo. Roberts, a Scottish painter, travelled throughout Spain, Morocco and Egypt and the result-ing albums of lithographs based on his drawings were published between 1842 and 1849. He had trained as a theatrical designer and brought precision and a Romantic sense of colour to his architectural renderings.

The most influential paintings of the Orient by Western artists originated in the eighteenth century. They initially consisted of landscapes, townscapes and views of prominent buildings, as did the extensive collection of paintings of India by William Daniell and his nephew Thomas. Soon after came interiors depicting Oriental social and religious life. A school of painting in France became known as the 'Orientalists'. In his book of the same name, sub-titled 'European Painters of Eastern Scenes', Philippe Jullian describes works that illustrate scenes from Spain to India. One of the most evocative is a watercolour by Eugène Delacroix of a Moorish interior which he painted on his travels in Morocco and North Africa. Some European artists like John Frederick Lewis lived for long periods in the Islamic communities they portrayed. Others, like Gérôme and Ingres, invented scenes of sensual delight intended to appeal to rich male collectors. The Orientalist painters rendered the architectural and decorative details both of interior and of exterior scenes. Such was the accuracy of these depictions that architects who had never visited those countries could create buildings in a convincingly Oriental style.

The most celebrated group of buildings in England in an exotic style was that constructed in the early nineteenth century for the Prince Regent at Brighton: the Royal Stables (now the Dome) and the Pavilion. Except for the interior of the Pavilion, which is Chinese in character, the archi-tecture of the ensemble was derived largely from Mogul India. The Mogul building that had, and still has, universal appeal is the Taj Mahal, the spec-tacular monument on the banks of the river Jumna at Agra, a timeless symbol of the loss of a beloved wife. The beauty of its form, its situation at the end of a formalized garden and the tragic circum-stances of its construction by the heartbroken

emperor invoked deep emotions of pleasure and sympathy. In the case of the Taj Mahal, it is the external composition of the domes and minarets that creates the memorable image. By contrast, it is the series of interior spaces and their incompa-rable proportions and intricately decorated surfaces that account for the aesthetic charms of the

other equally potent and celebrated symbol for Western taste. The exterior of the Alhambra Palace at Granada, although impressively sited, is simple and unexceptional. The overwhelming vision of interior courtyards, linked to fountains and gardens, aroused the perception of a garden of Paradise which is so vividly described in Sura 88 of the Holy Koran.

> On that day there shall be radiant faces of men, well pleased with their labours, in a lofty garden. There they shall hear no idle talk. A gushing fountain shall be there and raised soft couches with goblets placed before them; silken cushions ranged in order and carpets richly spread.

Measured drawings and engravings of the Alhambra Palace in Granada were published from the late eighteenth century onwards and these, associated with influences from Mogul India, were supplemented by stylistic elements from North Africa, Turkey and Persia, where religious and public buildings shared a common vocabulary of architectural style with the whole Islamic world. Eventually, taking certain Islamic design elements, Western designers developed a style that, although not completely homogeneous, possessed sufficient unifying characteristics to be recognizable as such. The use of intricately carved and moulded surfaces, often perforated and frequently decorated with coloured geometric patterns, distinguished it from revivals of former Western styles. For example, the use of domes with a particular profile, together with certain types of arch, such as the horseshoe arch, was distinct from the canons of medieval revivalism. The general impression of opulent pattern-making was augmented by carpets and textiles.

Lest it be assumed that this particular type of nostalgia is confined to Christians, a Muslim, Akbar Ahmed, has written at some length on what he terms the 'Andalus Syndrome'. He describes this in his book *Discovering Islam* as a yearning for past glories and refers to the Andalusian refugees in Morocco who had been expelled from Spain during the Christian Reconquest. They displayed the keys of their lost homes in Spain on their front doors as a symbol of the culture that they feared might disappear.

The music and poetry from the Moorish past has similarly inspired modern Spanish culture. In his *Nights in the Gardens of Spain* (1907) Manuel de Falla (1876–1946) paints a musical picture of the beauties of the gardens of Granada and Cordoba, and a contemporary group, Calamus, has made replicas of old Moorish instruments and performs songs and instrumental pieces of Arab Andalusian music. They have relied to a degree on the Andalusian tradition that survives in Morocco and other North African countries. Because of a similar respect for the era of *convivencia* (peaceful coexistence) in medieval Spain, when the discreet practice of the three religions of the 'Book' was tolerated in both Christian and Muslim areas, the Moorish style was adopted by many Jewish communities in the nineteenth and early twentieth centuries as suitable for the design of synagogues.

The term 'Moorish style' can be defined only loosely. The English word 'Moorish', the French 'Mauresque' and the Spanish 'Moro' are derived from the Greek word 'Mauros', meaning 'Eastern'. 'Oriental', or 'Eastern', is normally taken to include anything associated with the Far East, including China, Japan and Indonesia as well as those countries stretching from Morocco to India and is therefore not always synonymous with 'Moorish'. 'Moorish', on the other hand, never infers the cul-

This watercolour was painted by John Frederick Lewis when he was living in Cairo in the 1840s. Called *The Hhareem*, it is one of many similar pictures by him depicting harem life. The scene is set in the house he rented from the Coptic patriarch. The pasha is believed to be Lewis himself and the light-skinned lady on the right his wife Marian.

The fortified palace known as the Alhambra, which overlooks Granada, was constructed between the eleventh and fourteenth centuries. Built from red stone and clay, its name is derived from the Arabic word for red. The bold but simple exterior, set on a magnificent site, contained an extensive and luxurious residence for the Nasrid Kings. In the distance can be seen the first snows on the Sierra Nevada.

tures east of India. It is often applied more specifically in a geographical sense to those countries of North Africa presently called Morocco and Mauretania. From medieval times the term 'Moorish' was extended to include the Islamic culture of Al Andalus in Spain with those Muslims who opposed the Christian Crusaders in their attempts to recover the Holy Land. The term 'Saracen' was similarly used by Christians to describe a Muslim enemy and the adjective 'Saracenic', now little used, was later applied to Islamic architecture and its elements. 'Moorish style' is a Western concept and in its widest sense denotes a style derived from Islamic design elements found in countries ranging from Spain, in the West, to Mogul India, in the East. This is the sense in which it is used here.

The following chapters describe how Moorish style came into existence, how it developed into a Western mode of expression in architecture and the decorative arts, and how in the twentieth century it lives on, strongly in Islamic countries and more faintly in the West.

The Islamic religion spread rapidly eastwards from Arabia as far as Spain, where another pre-Islamic style was to influence Islamic design. This was the Visigothic style of church building, decoration and handicrafts. The Islamic state of Al Andalus evolved into the most cultured entity in Europe and produced its own characteristic architecture, of which the mosque in Cordoba and the later palace of the Alhambra in Granada are outstanding examples. Both the Christian and Jewish communities of Spain adopted some elements of Islamic style in their religious buildings. The style continued to develop along parallel lines in Morocco and Spain during the fourteenth century. Meanwhile the Fatimid dynasty in Egypt made sophisticated modifications to it in their religious and domestic buildings.

First the Persians and then the Ottomans of Turkey brought further elaboration to the decorative arts and architecture. Then the Moguls introduced these skills to India, where yet another version of the style was created with the incorporation of some features of the local Hindu style. Growing contacts between Europe and the Indian subcontinent stimulated Western interest in exotic Oriental forms during the sixteenth and seventeenth centuries, the Taj Mahal acting as the most powerful image.

Three chapters of this book are dedicated to a description and discussion of those factors of design that are essential to Moorish style. Architectural and decorative elements contain and define space. The visual experience of interior and

The Islamic rulers in Spain defended their frontiers with a network of fortresses. This illustration from a late tenth-century Mozarab manuscript, *El Comentario Al Apocalipsis* by Beato de Liebana, shows Saracen warriors in a state of readiness standing on the towers of a fort featuring characteristic horseshoe arches.

The south facade of the Taj Mahal reflected at dawn in one of the long pools in the symmetrical formal garden. The other side of the world's most celebrated tomb faces the river Jumna at Agra. The Taj was built by the Mogul emperor Shah Jehan to commemorate his wife Mumtaz Mahal who died in childbirth. It is said that it took 22 years to complete and provided employment for 20,000 workmen.

exterior spaces is determined by the arrangement of light-reflecting solids and voids. The horizontal and vertical elements of a building define spaces for human activities while the verticals also support any structure above. The voids provide natural lighting and views of the outside. Walls, arches, floors, windows, roofs and ceilings are shown to be used in ways representative of the style. The skilful employment of water and gardens, often accompanied by the sound of birds and fountains, produces an effect of peace and relaxation. The decorative treatment of surfaces, involving colour and almost unbelievably sophisticated systems of pattern-making, is a particularly important aspect of Moorish design, as are the arts of carpentry,

stonework, stuccowork and brickwork, ceramics, lapidary, glassmaking and metalwork, textiles, calligraphy and miniature painting.

Western fascination with Moorish style reached its zenith in the nineteenth century in the hands of Western designers. The revival of past style, initiated by the Italian Renaissance and continued in the neo-classical period of the eighteenth century was already well established. Looking beyond the Mediterranean to North Africa, the Near East and India, to borrow from the rich vocabulary of Islamic design, was the result of a desire for the exotic and the extravagant; Islamic design thus became another attractive item on the menu of available eclectic styles. It also coincided with the eastward

colonial expansion of Britain and France. The influence of Egypt and Mogul India coincided with the growing interest in Turkish and North African culture among European intellectuals. Famous literary figures conferred prestige on the Moorish style, especially the American writer Washington Irving, who visited the Alhambra in Granada in the early nineteenth century and returned with tales of its exotic nature and thrilling atmosphere. The publication of measured drawings of the Alhambra stimulated the imitation of its elaborate spaces in Europe and North America. Moorish style even reached Latin America, where the Mudéjar style, a Christian version of Islamic style, had travelled with skilled craftsmen from Spain.

The style underwent further development and variations in the twentieth century. By the turn of the century, Moorish style had been adopted in a wide variety of buildings, among them theatres, picture palaces, bullrings, exhibition halls and railway stations, where a sense of occasion was considered essential. Moorish design was also one of several sources of inspiration in the formation of both Art Nouveau in France and Modernismo in Spain. Similarly, many artists of the Modern Movement were affected by the abstract polychrome patterns they had seen on the surfaces of buildings in the Middle East.

As for those Islamic nations that have been so heavily influenced by predominant Western ideas

In 1826 the architect John Nash published a series of views of the Royal Pavilion, Brighton. This is a general view from the garden. Both the Pavilion and garden were commissioned by the Prince Regent who had developed a taste for the extravagant and the exotic. Nash's design for the palace's exterior is derived from Mogul architecture but the gardens are informal in character.

The interior of the Glock-
engasse Synagogue at Köln
was designed in the Moor-
ish style which many nineteenth-century Jews
believed to be the most
legitimate style, since it
was derived from the fourteenth-century synagogues
of Islamic Spain. Charac-
terized by a vivid use of
colour and intricate decoration, this example was
built in 1861. The architect
was Ernst Zwirner.

(largely brought to them by modern technology), the search for cultural identity has resulted in a number of buildings in a contemporary version of the Islamic tradition. Some of these have been designed by Western architects and as such could be seen as the latest examples of Moorish style. In Islamic countries, the tradition of decorative crafts survives, especially in Morocco, Egypt and Pakistan. Architectural design, by contrast, is in a state of transition, with varying degrees of Western influence and, on occasions, lack of refinement in the use of decorative skills. Perhaps the most significant recent event is the use of the computer in the creation of geometric and polychrome patterns of the Islamic vocabulary simultaneously by both Eastern and Western designers. In the late twentieth century, considerable interest in Moorish style persists in Europe and North America, although the use of that style is generally confined to buildings or interiors with a direct relevance to Islam or Islamic cultures.

Thus it appears that Moorish style actively lives on in both the West and the East. Its long and complicated history has a broad perspective. It has been shaped by four religions and a number of exceptional, sometimes eccentric, figures in the fields of religion, politics, literature and the visual arts. Examples of Moorish style vary in scale from small, exquisite objects to vast and imposing structures. Everyone, regardless of nationality, religion or background can appreciate them and admire their beauty. East and West have met and the interaction has produced a fascinating visual panoply.

This engraving, showing a performance of the American circus in the Alhambra Palace Music Hall in Leicester Square, appeared in the *Illustrated London News* of April 24 1858. The detailing of the interior was in the Moorish manner and included horseshoe arches. The central fountain of the building, which had previously been devoted to Science and Art, had recently been replaced with a circus ring.

Opposite: The Suleimaniye Mosque and its complex of tombs and educational buildings stands on a prominent site overlooking the Golden Horn at Istanbul. Designed by the great Ottoman architect Sinan for Suleiman the Magnificent, construction lasted from 1550 to 1557. This view from the tower of the Seraskier (Minister of War) is by William Henry Bartlett who travelled in Turkey and Lebanon and was the author of several albums of engravings in the 1840s and 50s.

Right: A glazed ceramic panel incorporating the coat of arms of Castile and Léon from the Casa de Pilatos in Seville. According to legend, this palace, which was built by Fadrique de Ribera in 1519 on his return from Jerusalem, is a copy of Pilate's house. It is planned around a central courtyard and uses a mixture of styles including Moorish.

A church, a temple, or a Ka'ba stone,
Koran or Bible or a martyr's bone,
All these and more my heart can tolerate,
Since my religion now is Love alone.
Al Maarri

Hagia Sophia, the Church of Divine Wisdom, stands in Istanbul as a monument to the Golden Age of the Byzantine Empire. Prominent are the huge buttresses and the semi-circular arch between them. The relatively shallow dome above also has a number of smaller buttresses. The four minarets were added later after the Ottoman conquest in 1453 when the church was converted into a mosque.

Many fundamental aspects of Moorish style are closely associated with the way of life of Islamic peoples and the canons of the Islamic religion. Some of those aspects, however, pre-date the foundation of the Islamic faith in AD 622. For example, certain features of Byzantine art and architecture provided both decorative and structural precedents for the designers and craftsmen who created the early Islamic buildings. Thanks to the stable construction and use of durable materials, many of these buildings have survived; thus the roots of Moorish style are still visible.

Perhaps the finest example of Byzantine architecture is the magnificent church of Hagia Sophia, in Istanbul. It was built in AD 532 on the orders of Emperor Justinian to the designs of Anthemius of Miletus. Occupying a spectacular site overlooking the Bosphorus, it is remarkable for the large-scale dome forming the roof over a huge square central space. The dome is supplemented on two sides by semi-domes to create a processional axis. Hagia Sophia demonstrates that the symbolic presence of a religious building can be emphasized by the silhouette of a dominant central dome. The dome subsequently inspired the designers of the Dome of the Rock in Jerusalem and the Ottoman

mosques of a later period. The dome has since assumed such symbolic importance in the world of Islam that its use in the design of mosques has become almost obligatory.

The characteristic form of a dome is normally obtained by assembling specially shaped stones and fitting them together in such a way that the weight of the stones above pushes downwards and outwards on the enclosing stones below. This exerts a considerable force, which pushes outwards at the lower edge, in addition to the downward gravitational force. The most stable form of dome is a hemisphere. Unfortunately, the original dome of Hagia Sophia was too shallow and so the weight at the centre created too much of a downward force, resulting in its collapse. It was then rebuilt to a deeper section, thus producing greater outward forces, which tended to make it spread at the base. These outward forces were restrained by the construction of gigantic buttresses. The dome, like an arch in three dimensions, depends on each block exerting a crushing or compressive stress on its neighbours. Stone, brick or concrete, being dense, effectively resist this kind of stress.

Another form of roof construction that takes advantage of the compressive strength of stone is the vault which is, in effect, an arch extended in a third direction. Arches can be round or pointed and are often used in areas where timber is scarce and stone or brick are freely available. Traditionally, however, timber is the principal material for beams and trusses because, being fibrous and pliable, it can withstand bending and tensile stress. On the other hand, as most timbers are less dense than stone or brick, they are less able to resist strong compressive forces. Timber was occasionally used in the construction of domes. The Dome of the Rock in Jerusalem is an example in which a series of frames were made in such a way that the timber

This lithograph of the interior of Hagia Sophia was made in 1852 by Giuseppe Fossati, a Swiss architect who had previously been engaged in the restoration work. His portrayal of the magical effect of the natural lighting and the vast scale of the interior space is marvellously realistic.

View through one of the pointed archways of the prayer space to the main courtyard of the Ibn Tulun Mosque at Cairo. The whole structure, which dates from 879, is made from red brick faced with stucco. The domed structure at the centre of the courtyard originally sheltered a fountain but the minaret is a later, probably thirteenth-century, addition.

base, allowing dramatic shafts of light streaming in from a lofty height to play across the wide floor of the church. The exterior was also dominated by arched openings, many of which illuminated the upper galleries and were integrated with the central dome and associated semi-domes.

The semicircular arch was later adopted by Islamic designers, appearing in many early buildings, from the Great Mosque in Damascus to the Alhambra in Granada, and subsequently in Ottoman mosques and palaces. It is now accepted as one of the key elements of Moorish style. But there is another type of arch that is usually considered to be more typical of the style. This is the horseshoe arch, examples of which occur in the Alhambra. During the nineteenth and early twentieth centuries, this arch was known in the West as the Saracenic arch. The setting-out of the arch is based on the circle but is nipped in slightly at the base to produce a horseshoe shape. Its origin is certainly pre-Islamic and examples have been traced in Syria and Ethiopia, as well as in several Visigothic churches. When the arch was developed for use in Islamic structures, the horseshoe shape was slightly more accentuated than in the Visigothic type, giving it a more pinched appearance.

members receive more tensile stresses than compressive ones.

The semicircular arch originated with the Romans and was characteristic of the Byzantine period. The Byzantine semicircular arch was built over openings in a flat wall or supported on capitals in turn placed on columns. These stone capitals were elaborately carved in relief, following a tracery pattern, and rested on columns of richly figured marble. The vast interior space of the great church of Hagia Sophia was dominated by the repeated use of the semicircular arch in flowing sequences at many levels and in a variety of sizes and scales. Four immense arches were used to support the central dome. A series of arched windows pierced the circumference of the dome

Another variation of the arch form that is found extensively in early Islamic buildings is the pointed arch. This was used in the Dome of the Rock and was an important element in the design of the mosque of Ibn Tulun at Cairo. It later became a characteristic motif of Persian and Mogul design. A pointed version of the horseshoe was common in North Africa and Spain, where it was often used to form single doorways in massive walled enclosures leading into cities, fortresses and palaces. One such example is the gate of Chella at Rabat. As the Islamic style developed, the desire for more

elaboration grew and further complications in the arrangement of the arch appeared.

Another important characteristic of Hagia Sophia that was to have influence in the subsequent formation of Islamic art was the widespread interior use of decorative mosaic panels. The effect of the glittering mosaics and the intricately carved latticework of the stone capitals topping the richly coloured marble columns was to create an impression of magical, soaring space that has rarely been matched since. It is not surprising, therefore, that, when the Dome of the Rock was built over the rock in Jerusalem whence Muslims believe the Prophet Mohammed ascended to heaven, the skills of the designer and craftsmen of Hagia Sophia were invoked. According to Ibn

Khaldoun, writing over 600 years later, Abdel Malik, the Umayyad caliph of Damascus, requested the Byzantine emperor to send craftsmen to Jerusalem to assist with the construction of the new mosque.

Islam did not immediately develop a distinctive architectural style for its mosques and other religious buildings. In fact, Muslims were content initially to adapt or even share existing churches and temples. Yet when they did build new mosques, two factors helped to create a stylistic difference between Muslim and Christian religious buildings. The first was the prohibition, in the Muslim faith, of any representation of humans in a religious building; the second was the absence of any need for a longitudinal axis, for a mosque is predominantly a space in which the congregation pray in

Above left: A simple horseshoe arch built in cut stone and set in a square recess with a flat relieving arch topped by accentuated voussoirs. This particular arch is from the tower of the church of San Sebastian in Ronda, Andalusia, which was formerly a minaret of the Nasrid dynasty.

Above right: A pointed horseshoe arch in cut red sandstone, also set in a square recession. This doorway is from Rabat in Morocco.

The exterior of the Dome of the Rock at Jerusalem boldly expresses the form of a dome sitting on a circular drum, which is in turn supported on an octagonal base. The dome is simply adorned with a golden skin, whereas above the window line the octagonal base is decorated with multi-coloured Turkish tiles. Below the window line the walls are lined with marble panels.

construction covered with gilt metal. It rises majestically on its drum over the octagonal base, the latter originally covered above the window line with glass mosaics representing trees, buildings and flowering plants. These exterior mosaics have since been replaced by sixteenth-century Turkish tiles. The interior mosaics, however, remain in their original glorious profusion of trees, scrolling vines, acanthus and vases of flowers with formalized curvilinear patterns. An inscription in gold on a blue background in a circular frieze at the base of the dome proclaims that Islam accepts the Prophets and Christ but not his divinity, emphasizing the oneness of God as opposed to the Trinity. It is the earliest example of Arabic calligraphy on a building. The lower mosaics are in blue and green set in a mother-of-pearl and gold background.

It is probable that Byzantine and Coptic craftsmen worked both on these impressive decorations and on those in the Great Mosque in Damascus. Al Walid I built this mosque within an enclosure that had been a Roman temple before it was converted into a Christian church. Only the four corner towers of the church were retained, becoming the prototype minarets for later mosques. The prayer hall, wider than it is deep, is approached through a large courtyard enclosed by a cloister on three sides. The central axis leads directly to the niche, or mihrab, which indicates the direction of Mecca. As Islam rapidly expanded west along the North African coast and east to Persia and India, this relatively simple layout was repeated again and again.

The westward movement of the Arabs to the Maghreb had been preceded by another march of conquest by the Visigoths, a Germanic people. As the Roman empire declined, the Visigoths moved along the northern shores of the Mediterranean from that part of the Balkans which is now Romania, to northern Italy. Later they established a king-

rows facing the direction of Holy Mecca, which is indicated by a niche in the wall. Unlike a Christian church, a mosque is not designed for liturgical procession and has no altar, sanctuary nor clergy. It is a unified space that makes no hierarchical distinction and is often wider than it is deep.

Both the Dome of the Rock in Jerusalem and the Great Mosque in Damascus demonstrate how the art and architecture of the mosque was formed and how it developed. In Jerusalem, Abdel Malik was at pains to make the shrine a powerful symbol of the new religion for both Christians and Jews. Because ambulation around the rock is an important part of Islamic ritual, as at the Ka'ba at Mecca, the mosque has a centralized plan with a prominent dome supported on a drum which is, in turn, supported on four piers and sixteen columns. This circular arrangement is contained within an ambulatory which is itself enclosed by the octagonal exterior wall. The dome, which was rebuilt in the eleventh century, is a double-skinned timber

Opposite: The interior surfaces of the dome and the circular drum of the Dome of the Rock are covered with splendidly patterned and coloured original mosaics. Vegetable motifs predominate and are accompanied by some of the first Arabic calligraphic inscriptions. The decorations owe much to pre-Islamic tradition and Byzantine skills.

Below: This Visigothic gold cross, inset with precious stones and dating from the seventh century, was found amongst other treasures at Guarrazar in the province of Toledo in 1853. Considered to have been offerings created in the royal workshops for the church of Toledo, these treasures show Byzantine influence.

dom in southwestern France and by the end of the fifth century they had occupied the greater part of the Iberian peninsula. As the seventh century drew to a close, a Christian Visigothic kingdom, with its capital at Toledo, was established in the peninsula south of the Pyrenees. The Visigoths developed a distinct artistic style of their own which resulted from a merging of the skills of this dominant Germanic group with the Hispano-Roman traditions of the majority of the native population.

A church at Quintinilla de las Viñas surviving from this period illustrates some of the features that are found later in Islamic style. The church, built well before the Moorish invasion of Spain in the eighth century, has a horseshoe arch, a feature that was to be characteristic of Islamic architecture. The horseshoe arch is both decorative and structurally functional. Other early examples have been found in Syria and a brick version dating from the fifth century has been excavated at Axum, in Ethiopia. The church at Quintinilla also has stone friezes carved in relief, which incorporate stylized representations of birds (peacocks and partridges) and vegetal themes (trees, leaves, grapes, vine tendrils and acanthus) in the form of medallions linked together within enclosing bands. These

Visigothic friezes show a high degree of skill and elegance of design; they have parallels in Byzantine and Coptic art of the same period and anticipate the use of friezes which was to become so prominent in Islamic architecture.

However, the Visigothic presence in Spain was short-lived. In 711 Abdel Tariq led an Islamic invasion which, because of the general unpopularity of the Visigoths, did not meet with fierce resistance. Very soon Seville, Cordoba and Toledo were occupied and by 714 both Huesca and Saragossa, in the north, had been captured. In time Cordoba became the centre of the Islamic part of the peninsula known as Al Andalus but dissension between the Arabs and the Berbers caused some unrest.

The golden age of Al Andalus began in 756 when Abder Rahman, the sole survivor of the Umayadd dynasty, was proclaimed Emir at Cordoba. During his reign Cordoba was famed for its support of the arts and culture. In 785 Abder Rahman decided to demolish the Christian cathedral in the centre of Cordoba which Christians had shared with Muslims. He then set to building the first phase of the Friday, or Great, Mosque, taking the Great Mosque in Damascus as the model for its layout. The simplicity of the interior of the prayer hall, with a mihrab, follows Damascus, although there are fundamental differences. At Cordoba directional emphasis is achieved with arcades of

Left: A carved stone frieze from an outside wall of the seventh-century Visigothic church at Quintinilla de las Viñas. The flowing circular tendril motif contains a variety of simple designs such as birds, grapes and shells. The horseshoe arch which stands in front of the sanctuary has carved stone decoration similar to that on the frieze.

shorter equal spans running parallel to the qibla, or central axis, whereas the arcades at Damascus are at right angles to the qibla. The interior becomes a magical forest of columns, the lower arcade, with horseshoe arches, surmounted by two superimposed arcades whose arches have alternate red brick and stone voussoirs. The lower arcade acts as bracing for the upper tiers of columns and there is open space above them, creating long diagonal perspectives of overlapping arches above endlessly repeating rows of columns. Here, perhaps, is the most memorable use of the horseshoe arch in any Moorish context.

Abder Rahman II extended the mosque in the ninth century, creating eight more bays to the south and thus making the prayer hall almost square in plan while maintaining the subtle repetitive simplicity of the first phase. Cordoba's continuing prosperity and expanding population made necessary a third extension to the mosque. This was undertaken by Al Hakam II between 961 and 976; an area equal to the original mosque was added on the south side, thereby introducing a sense of depth to the plan. With the construction of Al Hakam II's extension, a number of new architectural features were introduced: the trefoil arch, the multifoil arch, the pointed horseshoe arch, intersecting versions of the horseshoe and multifoil arches, three ribbed domes with a central octagon and a lantern ribbed dome with a central

square. Each of these features was subsequently adopted as typical devices in the Islamic building tradition. The upper parts of the mihrab wall were covered with gold mosaics ornamented with floral and vegetal motifs later known as arabesques. The mihrab arch was surmounted by angular Kufic calligraphy in gold on a blue background. Calligraphy was to become the supreme Islamic art form. In the Friday Mosque in Cordoba, Al Hakam II's designers and craftsmen set a standard of excellence in the integration of structure and magnificent decoration that was not to be matched until the time of the Nasrids in Granada. The building of the fourth and final extension of the Friday Mosque was undertaken in 987 in the reign of Hisham II by the chief minister, Al Mansour. One new feature introduced here, and apparently derived from Syria, was the pointed arch.

At the same time as developments took place under Umayyad rule in Cordoba, the Abbasids in Baghdad were using brick and stucco as their main materials for building and decoration. When Ibn Tulun became Governor of Egypt and Syria in 868, he introduced these materials in the construction of the mosque in Cairo that bears his name. This mosque has a severe and dignified aspect, with massive piers and pointed arches used both externally and internally. The basic structure is of fired

Right: A circular ivory casket elaborately carved with flowing arabesques into which images of peacocks and deer have been incorporated. There is a silver hinge and catch. This particular example comes from Madinat Al Zahra near Cordoba, where there was a royal workshop for making such caskets, and was made in 964 as a present for Subh (Dawn), a favourite of the Umayyad caliph, Al Hakam II.

Opposite: A view at right angles to the directional axis of the prayer space of the Great Mosque of Cordoba, showing the superimposed arcades which are composed of horseshoe arches below and semicircular arches above. The spaces between these two types of arches and the perspective of the repeating columns creates the impression of an endless forest stretching into the distance.

Right: The mihrab at Cordoba is highly ornate, providing an interesting contrast with the relatively simple main space of the mosque. The dome over the square bay in front of the mihrab serves to emphasize the direction of prayer. Based on the octagon and decorated with elaborate and colourful arabesques, the mihrab is framed by beautiful Kufic calligraphy in mosaic.

red brick faced with stucco incised with simple geometric patterns on the upper part of the walls. The parapet walls consist of an openwork frieze of merlons, a decorative finish which has now become a common feature of the domestic vernacular in the Middle East. The prayer hall is full of simple arcades running parallel to the mihrab wall. Later, in 1094, under the Fatimid dynasty the mihrab was framed with elaborate calligraphy carved in the stucco. This gave emphasis to the mihrab in contrast to the relative calm of its earlier decoration.

The Umayyadd dynasty in Al Andalus and North Africa gradually fell into decline. The Almoravids, a nomadic people, then rose to prominence and, by 1102, they ruled from the borders of Aragon to Senegal. Their puritanical outlook was shared by the Almohads, the dynasty that was to succeed them. The Almohads made Marrakesh, in Morocco, their capital and, crossing to Al Andalus, adopted Seville as their main base in the Iberian peninsula. Two fine minarets, at Marrakesh and Seville, typify the Almohads' attitude to public architecture. The minaret of the Koutoubia Mosque in Marrakesh is a tall tower built of local sandstone, square in plan and surmounted with a square domed lantern. Each face is different and each shows a wide variety of decoration and arch forms, although the minaret still exhibits a considerable degree of restraint. The famous minaret at Seville, designed by Ahmed Ibn Baso, who also designed the Marrakesh minaret, was completed in 1196. It is now known as La Giralda after the bronze statue of Faith acting as a windvane at the top of the elaborate lantern added in the sixteenth century to accommodate the bells of the cathedral which had replaced the Great Mosque. It is a noble and well-proportioned construction which reflects the Almohads' restrained, sensitive but imaginative taste.

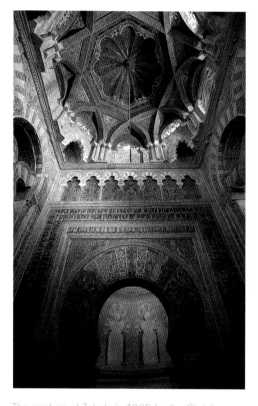

The capture of Toledo in 1085 by the Christians was not only important strategically, since it lies at the geographical centre of the Iberian peninsula and represented the southernmost extension of the Christian Reconquest (Huesca to the north was still in Muslim hands); it also had a strong religious importance, as Toledo had formerly been the Visigothic capital of Spain. The Muslims were permitted to keep their main mosque and were allowed religious freedom. There were restrictions on their employment but they were allowed to practise as masons, carpenters and plumbers as well as work in the leather and textile trades. Their expertise in agriculture and market gardening was essential to the development of the new Christian kingdom and they were encouraged to continue in these activities.

Overleaf: The main courtyard of the Mosque of Ibn Tulun in Cairo. The spiral minaret on the left is offset from the symmetrical axis of the mosque which is to the right of the picture. The continuous fretwork of the parapet wall contrasts with the dignified mass of the arcades below and the square domed structure with the fountain at its centre.

Above left: A capital from Santa Maria la Blanca. The design is based on stylized pine cones tied together with palm leaves.

Above right: The first volume of *España Artistica y Monumental* by Patricio de la Ecosura was published in 1842. This illustration shows the interior of the synagogue at Toledo, now known as Santa Maria la Blanca. Built in c.1200, it has five aisles divided by horseshoe arches.

Although it would seem that the Muslim presence in Toledo accounted for no more than five per cent of the total population of the city, influence in the shaping of urban architecture was considerable, and disproportionate to their numbers. However, as the Christian population in Toledo increased, there was an immediate demand for the conversion of mosques into churches. A surviving example of such a conversion is the church of Cristo de la Luz, which had been built as a mosque in 999. An apse was added in 1187 which followed the pattern of the original brick structure, with stone elements. The arcade and friezes of the mosque were continued in the design of the apse, creating a satisfying harmony between old and new. This church is probably the earliest example of what is now referred to as the Mudéjar style. The term is said to originate from the Arabic word '*mudayyan*', meaning 'those who have submitted'.

The position of the Muslims gradually became more difficult as they were seen increasingly as enemies within the Christian camp. The Jewish community, by contrast, was in a different situation as they had no assigned loyalty to an external enemy. Having royal approval, they flourished, especially in financial affairs. The Spanish Jews did not have an architectural heritage unique to them and were content to use the current forms for their own purposes, but they adapted them with great sophistication. A typical synagogue in Spain was a

El Tránsito, another synagogue in Toledo illustrated in Ecosura's book, was originally built by Mudéjar masons and carpenters in 1357 for Samuel Levi who was Treasurer to Pedro the Cruel of Castile. The rich decoration of the interior includes bands of Hebrew calligraphy. Subsequently converted for Christian use, the altar piece has now been removed and the building houses a museum of Hebrew culture.

A panel of glazed ceramic tiles from the Casa Pilatos in Seville displays the variety of colour and pattern inherent in the Moorish tradition. These tiles date from the sixteenth century.

relatively simple building, requiring no tall structure equivalent to a Christian bell tower or Muslim minaret. The main temple space was approached through a vestibule and was either simply rectangular or square in plan. It contained a raised dais with a lectern for the reading of the Torah, often set in the centre. The floor level of the synagogue was required to be no higher than street level, which helped to reduce the apparent external bulk of the building. The Talmud calls both for a ban on the representation of the human form and for the segregation of women in the place of worship. Two synagogues have survived in Toledo. One, dating from the twelfth century and now known as Santa Maria la Blanca, has five naves defined by horseshoe-arch arcades and the interior is richly decorated in the Mudéjar manner with a wealth of geometric patterning. A later and more splendid example, the Sinagoga del Tránsito, was built by Samuel Levi, the royal treasurer, in 1357. The interior is richly decorated and the stucco frieze is dedicated to Hebrew calligraphic inscriptions of the psalms punctuated with the coat of arms of the house of Castile.

During the thirteenth century Toledo developed into a prominent cultural centre. Much of the ancient knowledge of the Greeks and Romans had already been translated into Arabic when the Greek philosophers left Alexandria for Baghdad and Damascus. It was later absorbed into Andalu-

sian culture and translated into Latin. Alfonso X (the Wise), however, made Castilian the official Spanish language and founded the celebrated School of Translators. Knowledge of science, mathematics, astronomy, geography and medicine increased. Poetry and music also flourished. Alfonso wrote and set to music the celebrated *Cantigas de Santa María.* The importance of mathematics underlined the skill of Muslim craftsmen in the development of sophisticated geometric patterns in brickwork, glazed tiles, mosaic, stucco, timber and inlaid work of all kinds. Calligraphy, so important in Arabic Islamic culture, was extended to Hebrew, Latin and Castilian and was used for decorative inscriptions on public buildings. Outstanding skills in carpentry led to the development of the typical *artesonado* patterned ceilings, the most directly recognizable Mudéjar feature to survive in Spain after the expulsion of the Muslims. This was the embellishment of the system of carpentry supporting the roof above. This type of ceiling was employed in cathedrals, churches, palaces and important public buildings. Its widespread use was made possible by the presence in Spain of a number of skilled carpenters, some of whom could design complete buildings. A comprehensive knowledge of geometry was necessary and there were sourcebooks and written by-laws administered by master masons on behalf of the appropriate municipality. The sizing of the mem-

bers and the network of geometric patterns were decided according to accepted mathematical rules. In the field of pottery an expanding range of coloured glazes led to an increasing use of glazed tiles known as *azulejos*. As the name implies, these had originally been predominantly blue (azul).

To the east of Castile, however, the Christian kingdom of Aragon had also been expanding southwards. In spite of its northern location, Aragon, and the town of Saragossa in particular, had been strongly influenced by Islamic culture. There, the Muslim royal palace, the Aljafería, played a prominent role in the shaping of attitudes to design in the early phase of the Reconquest. It became the Alcázar (castle) of the Christian kings of Aragon and the richness of its interiors, particularly the former royal mosque, with its complicated use of surface patterns in a variety of materials, not only pleased the new occupants but set the standard by which new buildings were judged.

Sources of stone for building were not abundant in areas which had newly become part of Aragon, particularly the valley of the Ebro, and so the normal building material there was brick. Geometric patterns were created by the skilful manipulation of a standard brick called the *rejola*. It was twice as long as it was wide, theoretically two hands by one hand, and approximately 35.3 x 16.8 x 4.6 cm. The *rejola* was used in conjunction with a variety of special moulded bricks,

glazed tiles and medallions of green, purple and brown to give a richer and more elaborate effect, strong sunlight producing crisp shadows among the projecting bricks and giving life to the colours of the glazed tiles. So rich is the effect that some of the wall surfaces almost take on the appearance of huge hanging tapestries.

Teruel, however, is the town with the most spectacular display of Aragonese Mudéjar design. It was seen as the strategic key to the conquest of Valencia and the Levant, ideally placed to rid the eastern ports of the Muslims so that the Aragonese could set sail for Jerusalem on their Holy Crusade.

Teruel's five bell towers all have one characteristic in common: they were built over the street in such a way that the ground plan consists of two large pointed archways allowing passage through the tower, while the weight of the tower above is carried on two thick parallel walls. The towers rising over the archways are square in plan and decorated with rich brick patterning set off by coloured ceramic plaques, the colours ranging from red-brown to olive green and dark purple, depending on the additives used in the clay. Ceramic techniques had originally been introduced to Spain by the Arabs. The design of each tower is distinctive in its use of Mudéjar elements. The towers of St Martin and El Salvador are particularly striking and

Left: Another panel of ceramic tiles from the Casa Pilatos, which has a section of simple abstract geometric pattern used as a border.

Below: The chalice of St Dominic (Domingo) from the monastery of Santo Domingo de Silos in the province of Burgos. Moorish influence is evident in the style of the gold decoration. The monastery was rejuvenated and expanded by a twelfth-century monk who was subsequently canonized when the monastery was named after him.

Two arch forms from *Monuments in Spain and Portugal* (1892) by Constantin Uhde. The example above shows a superimposed brick arcade in which cusps have been introduced to the under surface or intrados of the pointed arches to give added visual interest. The lower example is an arcade in which semi-circular arches span between every other column and interlace, forming pointed arch forms at the under surface of each opening.

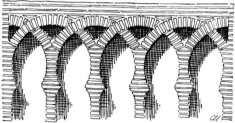

elegant in their height and proportions. The group of towers at Teruel gives the urban landscape an exotic, even Oriental, air.

All the colours used in the ceramic plaques of the Teruel towers are found in the pottery produced in the same workshops. Many of the scenes painted on the decorated plates and other ware of Teruel were based on the paintings on the *artesonado* ceiling of the cathedral. Among the motifs in these paintings are scenes of potters and painters, including their female assistants, at work as well as carpenters and wood carvers depicted in the very act of creating the roof structure and the ceiling itself. Monochrome architectural ceramics in the shapes found in Teruel had not previously been used in Al Andalus and so these have the stamp of originality.

The Marinids, the successors of the Almohads in North Africa, made the Moroccan city of Fez their capital. Alongside Old Fez, which had grown informally, the Marinids built a new city along planned lines. In New Fez many mosques and

madrassas (religious colleges) were constructed. The most important example is the Bou Inania *madrassa*, which, because it is also a mosque and a focal point for the religious hierarchy of the city, has a prominent minaret. This minaret overlooked all the others in Fez and, because there was an elaborate water clock nearby, an accurate time for prayer was easily co-ordinated from there. The *madrassa* was planned around a marble paved court with a central fountain. The prayer hall takes up one side of the court while the other three sides are bounded by cloisters supported on heavy piers. There is an entrance porch opposite the prayer hall and two square domed lecture halls at the centre of the other two sides. Student rooms face into the court at both ground- and first-floor levels, whereas the lecture halls rise through two storeys. Every surface of this magical building, from the tall minaret to the wooden screens of the student rooms, is impeccably divided into panels of elegant proportions and decorated with the full repertoire of Moorish skills. In the use of repetitive patterns worked into many contrasting materials, Andalusian luxury reasserted itself. The horseshoe arch is used in a vigorous pointed form to emphasize the entrance and qibla. Never before nor since have scholars and students enjoyed such a beautiful and peaceful environment for study and contemplation.

When the two kingdoms of Castile and Aragon were united by the marriage of Ferdinand and Isabella in 1469, the days of the Nasrid sultanate of Granada were numbered. The growing military power of the Christian kingdoms to the north had been anticipated and in the thirteenth century Mohammed I initiated the construction of a fortified palace on the Sabika hill above the city and his son Mohammed II completed the external walls. The fortifications were built from a mixture of red

Top left: La Giralda, Seville, is the minaret of the former mosque which has since been replaced with a Gothic cathedral. Renaissance features have now been added to house the bells and support the statue, which acts as the wind vane after which the tower is named. The rich geometric patterns of the decorative panels below survive from the twelfth century.

Top right: The stone minaret of the Koutoubia Mosque at Marrakesh, dating from 1147, is the precursor of La Giralda. Its faces are decorated with a variety of arch forms, of which the most prominent are the interlaced arches to the windows and niches. A horizontal band of blue-green glazed tiles runs round the parapet. The domed lantern was added in 1196.

Bottom left: The tower of San Martin in Teruel, Aragón, is dramatically placed to straddle the street. Built in 1315 in Mudéjar style, it is lavishly decorated with brick patterns and glazed ceramic plaques in green and white.

Bottom right: The tower of Teruel cathedral has similar Mudéjar decorations in brick and ceramic, with additional stone quoins and an octagonal lantern. It was built in 1257 and is the oldest of the Mudéjar towers of Teruel.

bra that the Western manifestation of Moorish style owes its existence.

Those parts of the Muslim palace that were added in the fourteenth century, first by Yusuf I and then by Mohammed V, have become legendary of a luxurious environment on a human scale. The Hall of the Ambassadors, the Courtyard of the Myrtles and their subsidiary spaces are usually known collectively as the Comares Palace and were completed in the time of Yusuf I. The contiguous suite of spaces centred around the Court of the Lions was built by Mohammed V, probably for his personal use and for that of his family. The Fountain of the Lions, after which the courtyard was named, is inscribed around the basin with a series of verses in praise of Mohammed V. One verse reads:

> Blessed be He who gave the Imam
>   Muhammed a mansion which in beauty
>   exceeds all other mansions....
> Here is the garden containing wonders of
>   art the like of which God forbids should
>   elsewhere be found.
> Look at this solid mass of pearl glistening
>   all around and spreading through the air its
>   showers of prismatic bubbles.
> While it falls within a circle of silvery froth,
>   and then flows amid other jewels surpassing
>   everything in beauty even exceeding the
>   marble itself in whiteness and transparency.

These and other verses inscribed in the calligraphic friezes found in many of the rooms in the Alhambra are attributed to Ibn Zamrak who, as well as being chief minister to Mohammed V, was a poet.

The plainness of the Alhambra's exterior, appropriate to a fortress, contrasts so dramatically with the lavish and sophisticated interiors and the

earth and stone with a strong red colour, hence the name Alhambra ('the red' in Arabic). The world-renowned palace quarters were built in stages within the walls and became a settlement in their own right with a mosque, a public bath and a market independent of the royal quarters. It is these royal quarters that have come to be regarded as the most beautiful and most sensitively conceived royal palace in the world. From the eighteenth century onwards, the Alhambra has been a source of inspiration for countless European and American poets, writers, painters and composers, including, in the twentieth century, the Andalusian composer Manuel de Falla and the poet Federico García Lorca. It is now the most celebrated tourist attraction in Spain, and, to a large extent, it is to the rediscovery of the Alham-

The Alcázar is the royal palace rebuilt in Seville for King Pedro the Cruel of Castile at the same time as Mohammed V was making his additions to the Alhambra. This is a view of the archway in the Hall of the Ambassadors which combines a dado of coloured glazed tiles with intricately carved stucco to the surfaces above in a similar manner to many of the apartments in the Alhambra.

Above left: The domed ceiling to the Hall of the Ambassadors in the Alcázar at Seville was added in 1427 and is the masterpiece of Diego Ruiz. It is made of interlocking timber sections with complicated geometric patterns which catch and reflect the light, suggesting the stars in the heavens.

perfumed charm of the gardens that its magic is pervading and persistent. The Nasrids had encouraged the established pottery industry to extend the wide range of its glazed tiles, which already featured *cuerda seca* decoration, its lustreware and its innumerable coloured glazes. The repertoire of construction and decoration, brought to a state of near-perfection at the Bou Inania *madrassa* at Fez, is taken a stage further at the Alhambra, especially in the range of ceiling designs. Here the *muqarna*, a device originally developed to aid the transition from walls on a square plan to a circular dome above, appears as a small three-dimensional unit which recurs to form a richly moulded and carved repetitive pattern. There are many examples, both in finely carved stucco and almost unbelievably complex marquetry. But perhaps the most unusual ceilings are those in three alcoves in the Hall of the Kings, which have colourful portraits on leather of a series of Islamic dignitaries.

Mohammed V's additions to the Alhambra were contemporaneous with new developments within the Alcázar palace at Seville undertaken for

Pedro I of Castile. These monarchs were reputed to be friends and it is thought that Muslim craftsmen from Granada worked on both projects. Although many alterations and additions have been made since Pedro's time, much still remains of what was the most magnificent palace in the Mudéjar style. At the Alcázar Pedro reconstructed the Hall of Justice next to the Patio del Yeso, which had been built by the Almohads, but the main centre of his new palace, where he lived with his mistress, María de Padilla, was the Patio de las Doncellas (Court of the Maids of Honour). Two storeys of royal apartments were arranged around this court, including the Hall of the Ambassadors and a smaller courtyard known as the Patio de las Muñecas (Court of the Dolls). The main facade to the entrance courtyard, ornamented with arabesque themes, is divided into three and the entrance doorway at the centre has angled overhanging eaves at first-floor roof level. Just below the central projecting eaves is a horizontal panel in blue-and-white glazed tiles which displays the motto of Mohammed V repeated in geometric

Above centre: The Hall of the Ambassadors at the Alhambra has a sloping ceiling consisting of three planes to each side of the square plan. It is another masterpiece of marquetry and is made from over 8,000 polygonal wooden pieces. Dating from the early fourteenth century, this ceiling was the prototype for subsequent *artesonado* ceilings. The geometrical twelve-sided star patterns again represent the heavens, while the square flat central section at the summit serves as an image of the throne of Allah.

Above right: A detail of a timber ceiling in the Alcázar whose design is based on a square unit containing a sixteen-sided star motif which forms an octagonal star at each corner junction.

The Hall of the Ambassadors has a remarkable timber ceiling of interlocking faceted pieces in star-shaped patterns which was added in 1427. As at the Alhambra, a multiplicity of *muqarnas* was used to effect the transition between the dome and the square plan of the earlier construction below. Andalusian art, which is mainly Muslim in derivation, was now benefiting from Muslim, Christian and Jewish patronage (at least in the Iberian Peninsula), which produced supreme quality and beauty. The two palaces at Granada and Seville are the fruit of an artistic *convivencia* (harmonious cohabitation) which was later to dissolve into mutual distrust and, ultimately, hostility.

Islamic art had also been disseminated elsewhere. The Fatimids, who belonged to the Shi'a faction of Islam, moved east from Qairouan, conquered Egypt and made Cairo their capital, where they built the Al Azhar mosque in 972. According to a drawing made by Creswell in 1951, the mosque, which incorporated a university, was built of brick with keel arches (a form of pointed arch shaped by arcs described from two centres with the inner curve almost a straight line) supported on salvaged stone capitals and columns. It was extensively reconstructed at the end of the nineteenth century but the overall design and the details of the original work owe much to the precedent of the mosque of Ibn Tulun, especially the curvilinear stucco ornament of the mihrab. The Fatimids brought with them to Egypt particular skills of glass-making and some beautiful examples of lustre decoration on glass have survived.

A later dynasty, the Mamlouks, were great builders. The large mosque at the western foot of the citadel of Cairo begun by Sultan Hassan in 1356 was unfinished at the time of his death in 1362 and much of the decoration is still incomplete today. His mausoleum was the first to be

Kufic script. It reads: 'There is no victor but Allah'. Below this panel there are multi-lobed arcaded windows at first-floor level above the entrance. Yet another inscription visible on the facade, which consists of an enthusiastic paean of praise for Pedro, commemorates the date of his reconstruction of the palace, 1364.

The impressively tall entrance to the mosque of Sultan Hassan in Cairo, as depicted in an 1840s lithograph by Louis Haghe after David Roberts. The porch has a ceiling of elaborate *muqarnas* and is approached by a flight of steps to the general level of the mosque complex, which is well above street level. The vast scale of the mosque, which adjoins the Sultan's tomb and several *madrassas*, is intended to symbolize the power of the Mamlouk dynasty.

This oil painting by John Frederick Lewis is one of his last works and dates from 1872. It represents a crowded scene in the Bezestein Bazaar of El Khan Khalil in Cairo. The skilful rendering of the bright reds and blues of the costumes against the gloomy background of the covered bazaar and the brilliance of the lofty skylights gives a magical impression of both animation and coolness.

The dome of the Selimiye
Mosque at Edirne (Adri-
anople) is the largest of all
the Ottoman domes. The
mosque was designed for
Selim II in 1569 by Sinan
when he was nearly eighty
and it is generally considered to be his masterpiece.
This view shows the generous lighting of the interior
and the ornate mimbar
carved in marble. On the
left is a raised platform
used for singing and below
it a small fountain.

attached to a mosque and an enormous complex resulted, including a *madrassa* and ancillary accommodation. The domed tomb of the founder, on the main axis behind the mihrab, is flanked by two minarets. The dome, thought to have been wooden and in an onion shape, collapsed in 1661 and was replaced by a pointed stone structure. A magnificent central courtyard on a cruciform plan, another innovation, with lofty walls and a fountain on the axes of the four prayer spaces, creates an overwhelming impression of space. Many superb gilt and coloured glass mosque lamps, especially made for the building, hang from the ceiling. Four *madrassas*, one for each of the schools of Islamic law, occupy the four external angles of the mosque. The street entrance consists of a *muqarna* porch thirty-seven metres high, leading to a domed vestibule giving indirect access to the mosque interior. The huge scale was intended to impress the citizens with the glory of Allah and the Sultan. It also reflected the importance of Cairo as an international centre of commerce.

Under the Mamlouks, the domestic architecture of the growing merchant class was to reach a high degree of sophistication and the Mamlouk house was to remain the standard type in Cairo until the late nineteenth century, in spite of Ottoman rule and influence. The typical two- or three-storey courtyard house was developed to accommodate the extended family and the business needs of the merchant. These interiors were later to fascinate European visitors, especially those who spent long periods living in Cairo. In the early nineteenth century E W Lane described in graphic prose the houses and the way of life of the urban middle class. Similarly, the painter Frederick Lewis depicted the luxurious interiors and streetscapes of Cairo, in glowing watercolours and oils. Interior scenes of families, with graceful ladies reclining on rich

coloured textiles before alcoves lit through elaborate *mashrabiyya* windows attracted enthusiastic crowds when they were exhibited in the 1850s at the Old Watercolour Society in London.

The Ottomans developed a characteristic style of architecture and decoration which found full expression after Constantinople became the capital of the Ottoman empire. Hagia Sophia was converted into the chief mosque of the conqueror Mehmet II. A galaxy of new mosques was soon to be built. The Suleimaniye Mosque, built over a century later, is probably the most magnificent and is the centre of a large complex which comprises a medical college, a hospital, four other colleges, a hostel, a refectory, and a college for advanced studies. The mosque is approached through the customary ablution court and its plan, with a huge central dome and two semi-domes on the axis of the mihrab, owes much to Hagia Sophia. A separate tomb for Suleiman was placed behind the mihrab, also on the main axis. The complex was designed by Sinan, architect to the Sultan, under whose supervision countless buildings throughout the empire were designed and erected.

The outline at dawn of the Suleimaniye Mosque complex in Istanbul. An instantly recognizable symbol of Islamic architecture, the familiar shape of the dome combines with the tall elegant form of the minarets.

The characteristic external form of an Ottoman mosque is a large central dome with sub- or semi-domes; the smaller ancillary spaces are roofed with a series of small-scale domes. All the domes are roofed with lead and there are inevitably one or more tall, elegant free-standing cylindrical minarets. The internal structure of the prayer hall is simply articulated, and decorated with glazed tiles and coloured inserts in the predominantly clear-glass windows. The Suleimaniye Mosque has large calligraphic roundels designed by Karahisari, the most accomplished of the many calligraphers at the imperial court. Here, for the first time, Iznik tiles were introduced in their beautiful clear reds, greens, blues and white. Embodying flowing floral patterns, they were to become an essential element in the decoration of royal and religious build-ings. The tulip, the most famous Iznik motif, appears frequently in the tiles used in the Topkapi Sarai. Walls, ceilings and the inner surface of domes were painted and gilded in elegant, non-figurative recurring patterns, often arranged in panels. These patterns were also reflected in the carpets and prayer rugs which covered the floors of mosques and palaces. Turkish textiles became rich in colour, pattern and texture, thus placing great emphasis on the floor — a natural emphasis since prayer was performed and most social activi-ties took place at this level. If any stools or cush-ions were used for comfort, they were usually confined to the margins of the room.

The arrival of the Mongols in Persia in the early thirteenth century had initially had destructive consequences. After their conversion to Islam, however, they began to build with fervour. Since the Mongol empire stretched eastwards to China, there was an interchange of cultural ideas that had a strong bearing on the arts. The emphasis on structure that had been present under the Seljuks

was gradually replaced by a greater interest in ornamental surface. Walls were built of rubble and covered with coatings of stucco incised with pat-terns, while domes became higher and lighter. Advances were made in the production of glazed tiles, particularly in the development of rich turquoise and dark blue glazes on tiles that were sometimes embellished with real gold. The tech-nique of lustre painting was also introduced.

Later in the sixteenth century, the Safavid dynasty firmly placed Persia in the Shi'ite faction of Islam, where it has remained ever since. Architec-ture and the decorative arts flourished and in 1598 Shah Abbas I decided to transform Isfahan into a new capital with a vast open space, known as the Meidan-i-Shah, at its centre. The magnifi-cent mosque of Shaykh Lutfullah was reserved for the Shah's private worship; another, larger mosque for public worship, the Masjid-i-Shah, was con-structed between 1611 and 1638. Both these impressive buildings have tall portals facing the Meidan. At Isfahan, the external use of coloured tile mosaic reached its apogee. Although the portal of the Masjid-i-Shah faces north and is perma-nently shaded, the predominantly blue tiles gleam with a special intensity. The pointed and slightly bulbous dome of the mosque, together with its drum, is covered with a mosaic of turquoise and blue tiles with an elegant pattern of arabesques and calligraphy. The mosque's two tall cylindrical minarets are similar in form to Ottoman examples but covered with a predominantly turquoise tile mosaic with rectangular geometric patterns deftly arranged on the curved surfaces. The apex is ter-minated with a small dome, unlike the sharp coni-cal finish of the Ottoman minaret. Compared with the restrained exterior stone surfaces of Turkish mosques, those in Isfahan show a confident and integrated display of bright colour, pattern and calligraphy that is unequalled elsewhere. Bold use of colour and pattern on the exterior of buildings is rarely attempted in more northern cultures, where the lack of strong sunlight, and therefore of crisp shadow, and the damaging effects of a wetter climate encourage the use of monochrome or more restrained treatments.

In striking contrast to the extrovert glories of the mosques, the royal palace at Isfahan, like the Alhambra, was introvert and relatively modest, achieving a harmonious balance between interior and exterior space through the subtle placement of fountains and water which reflect the charms of the garden. These and other similar environments were the subjects of miniature paintings illustrating the relaxed domestic life of the Shah and his courtiers. Wall paintings in the local style of the miniatures included a number of figures in European dress, indicating that Western visitors had beheld at first hand the splendours of Persia. Further evidence of this are the Oriental textiles and carpets with which they returned and which soon became items of prestige in prosperous European households.

The confrontation between the Ottoman empire and Christian Europe hastened the end of the *convivencia* under which the presence of Muslims and Jews was accepted in those parts of Spain that had been reconquered by the Christians. The Inquisition, moreover, encouraged intolerance. Finally the hostility of the Church and the middle class compelled Philip III of Spain to issue a series of decrees between 1609 and 1614 confirming that remaining Muslims should be expelled. A few were allowed to stay, under strict conditions which included a ban on the use of the Arabic language and the wearing of Moorish clothes. The Jews had already been expelled in 1492, with a consequent loss of skills in the financial and pro-

fessional sectors of the economy. From 1614, Spain had ostensibly achieved *limpieza de sangre* ('cleansing of blood', which some today would equate with ethnic cleansing), but at a great cost both to its economy and culture.

After 1609 at least 70,000 Muslims, who had inhabited the rich irrigated lands of the Ebro valley in Aragon, left Spain and found their way to Tunis. The élite stayed in the city, where there is a street in the medina known as the Street of the Andalusians. The farmers moved to districts where conditions were similar to those that they had left behind in Aragon. The craftsmen took with them skills of silk-weaving and pottery-making, as well as building. There are two towns in Tunisia, Tozeur and Testour, where evidence of Aragonese expertise still survives. The older district of Tozeur has an urban environment similar to parts of Teruel or Calatayud and many buildings are in Mudéjar style. The minaret of the main mosque is octagonal in plan and appears to have lost its former decoration of ceramic tiles. It could nevertheless be mistaken for an Aragonese bell tower. Inside, the mihrab is richly decorated with star patterns, brick pillars and intricately carved woodwork. In Testour, the Friday Mosque, which was built in the seventeenth century, has a minaret on a square plan but it is surmounted by an octagonal tower and lantern. This minaret is also similar to an Aragonese bell tower, but for the fact that it has fewer openings at a high level since no bells were required. The plan of the main body of the mosque follows the traditional Islamic form in that it is wider than it is deep and is approached through an open courtyard with arcades on three sides. The decorative form of the shell was used over the mihrab, as well as on the supports to the dome above. This is unusual in a mosque, and is attributed to Spanish influence.

This coloured lithograph from *Monuments Modernes de la Perse* (1856) by Pascal Xavier Coste, shows the wide courtyard facing the main portal of the domed prayer hall of the Shah's Mosque at Isfahan.

Meanwhile, further east, the first Mogul emperor, Babur, a descendant of Timur-lane, crossed the north-west frontier from Kabul into India, leaving behind a cool climate and a court life that owed much to Persian cultural sophistication. He was a warrior intent on conquest and was later to found an empire that would occupy almost the whole of the Indian peninsula from Kashmir southwards beyond Madras. He captured Delhi and Agra, where he settled and made a traditional Islamic garden. The Moguls combined military skill with extensive and enlightened patronage of the arts. It was at Agra that Akbar, the greatest of the Moguls, built a fort of red sandstone which he made his main base and where he held a daily public audience in the meeting-hall. The more private apartments, built by local Hindu craftsmen, were developed nearby to take advantage of the river breezes. Like Babur, Akbar loved nature and created gardens on the riverside, where he was eventually buried. But the most extensive of his projects was the new city of Fatehpur Sikri. Akbar had no son but innumerable daughters, and so was astounded when a holy man predicted that he

would have three sons. The next year his Hindu wife became pregnant and was sent to Sikri, where she gave birth to Akbar's first son. When a second son followed, Akbar decided to build a new city near the holy man's hermitage, in celebration. This city was to become the cultural and administrative centre of India but was in fact occupied for only fourteen years before being abandoned because, so it is said, of a shortage of water.

This remarkable monument remains virtually unchanged to this day. It was built from local sandstone and marble cut with great precision and lightness of touch and includes many ornamental perforated window grilles. The palace buildings consist of a series of pavilions with wide overhanging eaves. The upper floors are often only balustraded platforms supported on slender columns, the highest surmounted by domes and overhanging eaves. Akbar established an imperial library, in spite of being illiterate and having to rely on readers. Miniature painting was encouraged and, under his supervision, a Mogul style was developed from a fusion of Persian, Hindu and European influences. While at Fatehpur, Akbar proclaimed a new religion that comprised ideas from Islam, Hinduism, Jainism, Zoroastrianism and even a few from Christianity and sun worship. The design of the Diwan-i-Khas, his private audience hall, symbolizes his view of his central position as ruler of the four quarters of his empire and, like other buildings at Fatehpur, shows Hindu influence in the design and carving of the details. It is a square pavilion with a central column that supports a circular platform on elaborate cantilevered stone brackets arranged like the spokes of a wheel. Four bridges connect the platform to a surrounding passage for access and to an external balcony. Here Akbar must have reclined in splendour, attending to affairs of state.

Opposite: Four close-up views of the Shah's mosque at Isfahan. The mosque is a dominant feature of the new capital which was created at the beginning of the seventeenth century by Shah Abbas I between the old town and the Zayandeh river. It has a grand entrance portal facing the Meidan, the vast central space of the capital, but the main portal of the mosque opens off the courtyard whose axis is diagonal to the Meidan.

Top left: Close-up of the main portal between the two minarets.

Top right: Detail of the luxuriant glazed ceramic tiling, showing the use of contrasting colours and patterns. The almost abstract geometrical Kufic calligraphy on the base of the minaret is particularly striking.

Bottom left: Close-up of the two-storey arcade in the courtyard.

Bottom right: Detail of the ceramic decoration to the blind arches and window grilles.

A Mogul miniature showing
the Emperor Akbar super-
vising the construction of
his new capital at Fatehpur
Sikri in 1571. He is at the
top of the picture accom-
panied by two servants,
one of whom is holding a
fan. This miniature is one
of many which appear in
an album called *Akbarna-
ma*, an official history of
his reign.

The most famous Mogul building of all is, of course, the Taj Mahal, an image familiar to millions of people throughout the world. Shah Jehan, Akbar's grandson, lost his wife Mumtaz Mahal, in childbirth and was so heartbroken that he went into mourning for two years. He then created a mausoleum for her on the banks of the river Jumna. The tomb forms the focal point at the end of the main axis of a great formal Islamic paradise garden, divided into the traditional four quarters, with water and trees (see page 16). It is raised on a terrace with four minarets placed symmetrically about it. The dominant central dome, bulbous in the manner of the Persian form, is enclosed at the four corners with four smaller domes placed on open arched octagonal pavilions. The main structure is square in plan, with splayed corners, and pierced by pointed arches on two levels, except at the entrance porch on the main axis, which rises the full height. The entire building is sheathed in translucent white marble, largely without intrusive

embellishment, which gives it a magical luminosity and coloration that varies from blue to white to golden yellow according to the time of day. To see the Taj Mahal reflected in the lake at sunrise or sunset is an experience without parallel.

Both Mumtaz and Shah Jehan lie buried here, their memorials enclosed within an exquisite trellis screen carved from marble. There is considerable but restrained ornamentation both inside and outside the building in the form of slender inlaid arabesques of coloured marble, as

well as long Koranic inscriptions in black marble. The skills of Mogul craftsmen at intricate marble inlay survive today. The identity of the architect or designer of the Taj Mahal is uncertain, although much was written by travellers of the splendours of the Mogul court at that time. Shah Jehan continued to indulge his passion for building by establishing a new capital at Shahjahan-abad, now known as Old Delhi. European interest in Mogul culture was to grow from the seventeenth century onwards, eventual invasion and occupation taking place in the eighteenth century.

Below: The Diwan-i-Khas, or private audience hall, at Fatehpur Sikri contains a single central pillar supporting a circular platform on which Akbar sat as if presiding between heaven and earth. This and other buildings at Fatehpur Sikri were built in red sandstone by Hindu masons who used a sophisticated technology derived from local traditions of joinery.

Above: The sarcophagi of Shah Jehan and his wife Mumtaz lie side by side in an octagonal enclosure consisting of pierced marble screens inlaid with precious stones. They are placed at the very centre of the Taj Mahal complex at Agra. The contrast of the incredibly delicate geometry of the screens with the floral designs on the floor is emphasized by the pattern of light and shade.

Opposite: An official visitor to the royal palace of the Alhambra at Granada would have relaxed in the Court of the Myrtles before being called to the Hall of the Ambassadors for an audience.

Right: A member of the congregation passing through the entrance court on his way to pray at the tenth-century Karaouine mosque in Fez, Morocco.

Know that the world is a mirror from head to foot,
In every atom are a hundred blazing suns,
If you cleave the heart of one drop of water,
A hundred pure oceans emerge from it.
Mahmud Shabistari

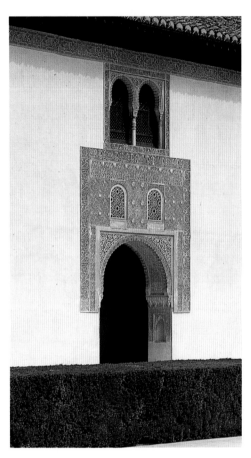

An opening in the long flank wall of the Court of the Myrtles at the Alhambra. Both the square frame to the semi-circular arch and the surrounds to the twin-arched openings above are richly decorated with carved stucco ornament to give emphasis in the plain wall surface. The trimmed hedge of myrtle is reflected in the pool.

In order to understand how a range of space elements in the Islamic architectural tradition would have been perceived by a visitor to a particular building, let us imagine the visit of a prominent delegate to the Palace of the Alhambra during its heyday in the fourteenth century. Let us assume that our visitor was seeking an audience with the Sultan. Let us try to picture his impressions as he awaited an audience relaxing on cushions and carpets in the shade on the south side of the Court of Myrtles. He would have been fascinated by the ceaseless play of sunlight on the jet of water from the fountain. His gaze would have been drawn to the sparkling reflections from the water as it rose

in the air to fall in glistening droplets and flow gently along the marble channel before returning to the placid waters of the long rectangular pool. Reflected in the pool and situated at the far end of the courtyard was an arcade of seven archways. The visitor would also have kept his eye on the larger central arch, waiting for the summons to the royal presence, because beyond this arch lay the entrance to the Hall of the Blessing, which acted as the vestibule of the Hall of the Ambassadors, where royal audiences were held.

The enjoyment of the tranquillity and visual beauty of this enclosed space depended on the delegate's perception of the light reflected from the enclosing surfaces and objects within. His direct perception of the form and rhythm of the arcade would have been supplemented by a second, inverted image created by rays of light from the arcade falling on to the surface of the pool. Whenever his attention strayed, unless he looked directly up to the sky, he would not have been able to see beyond the courtyard because of the lack of any openings in the enclosing walls but his total visual experience would have been enhanced by the play of sunlight.

Eventually the delegate would have been summoned to the Hall of the Ambassadors, where the Sultan would have received him. Inscriptions over the three windows in the north wall declare:

Long may you live! Thus when you enter in
   mornings and evenings, the mouths of
   boon, bliss, felicity and charm greet you
   in my name,
She is the high-domed hall and we are
   her daughters, however, mine is the pre-
   eminence and the honour in rank,
We are members among which I am the
   heart, unchallenged, for the power of spirit

An illustration by Owen Jones and Jules Goury showing the view of the Court of the Myrtles from the Hall of the Ambassadors. The elaborate carved stucco *muqarnas* that decorate the arched opening have been drawn in meticulous detail. The geometric patterns of the ceramic dado and the floor of the hall are also clearly discernible.

Above left: An elevational drawing by Christian Ewert of the west arcade of the bay in the Great Mosque at Cordoba shown in the illustration opposite. Here simple horseshoe arches are interlaced with multi-lobed arches which bear on the multi-lobed arches below.

Above right: At the Aljafería, a fortified palace in Saragossa, in the north portico to the main court-yard there are arcades of multi-lobed arches, some of which are also interlacing. To the right is the entrance to the prayer hall. These examples of compli-cated carved stucco date from the eleventh century when Saragossa was the capital of an independent Muslim kingdom.

and soul originates in the heart.
And if my symbols represent the constellations of her heaven, then in me, and not among them, is the grandeur of the sun.
My master Yusuf has decked me (may God support him!) in garments of pride and flawless artistry.
He made me the seat of the kingdom and thus she has strengthened his rank with the true light, with the seat and the throne.

In the Hall of the Ambassadors the delegate would have found a lower level of daylight because no direct sunlight could enter, only diffused light through window grilles set high in the walls and through deep arched openings at ground level. These lower openings gave panoramic views of the river valley and the city below and of the mountains beyond. Having travelled 75,000 miles all over the world and having visited Egypt, India and China, Ibn Battuta, a celebrated traveller of the time, wrote 'these environs have not their

equal in any country in the world. They extend for the space of forty miles and are traversed by the river of Shannil and many other streams. Around it on every side are orchards, gardens, flowery meadows, noble buildings and vineyards. One of the most beautiful places there, is Ayn ad Dama (Fountain of Tears) which is a hill covered with gardens and orchards and has no parallel in any other country.'

Having admired the panorama below, the visi-tor would then have turned his attention to the Sultan and his courtiers, whose rich and luxurious costumes complemented the intricately carved and multicoloured surfaces of the walls behind them. He would have been aware of the sunlit walls, floors and domed ceiling, which varied in pattern and intensity of tone according to the size, shape, proportion and position of the window openings. The arches surmounting the openings were all semicircular.

At the palace of the Aljafería in Saragossa, arches were interlaced in such a way that they

Opposite: The Great Mosque at Cordoba also has a series of multi-lobed arcades. These are found in the central bay in front of the mihrab in that sec-tion of the mosque built in the time of Al Hakam II.

A photograph of the interior of the Pearl Mosque at Agra from *Picturesque India* (1928). The multi-lobed arches are carved from translucent marble. The praying figure is facing the mihrab which is just out of sight on the left.

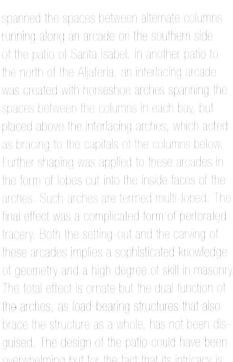

spanned the spaces between alternate columns running along an arcade on the southern side of the patio of Santa Isabel. In another patio to the north of the Aljaferia, an interlacing arcade was created with horseshoe arches spanning the spaces between the columns in each bay, but placed above the interlacing arches, which acted as bracing to the capitals of the columns below. Further shaping was applied to these arcades in the form of lobes cut into the inside faces of the arches. Such arches are termed multi-lobed. The final effect was a complicated form of perforated tracery. Both the setting-out and the carving of these arcades implies a sophisticated knowledge of geometry and a high degree of skill in masonry. The total effect is ornate but the dual function of the arches, as load-bearing structures that also brace the structure as a whole, has not been disguised. The design of the patio could have been overwhelming but for the fact that its intricacy is

counterbalanced by the simplicity of the pool and the layout of the garden.

Multi-lobed arches were also featured in buildings of the Nasrid period. A celebrated example is the courtyard of the Maids of Honour in the Alcázar at Seville, where the arches appear in arcades and are supported on pairs of slender marble columns. The most extensive use of this type of arch was in India where the Mogul designers displayed a preference for it in many prominent buildings, such as the Pearl Mosque at Agra and the Red Fort at Delhi.

The view of outside space, as seen through an arcade, is defined by the arches and their supporting columns or piers, each opening acting as a frame. The total perception might be of a series of framed views and the intention of the Islamic designers and craftsmen was to impart richness to the scene by adding carving and elaboration to the voussoirs (the tapered stones forming the arch).

Above left: A perspective of simple whitewashed and pointed horseshoe arches, looking across the prayer space of the Koutoubia Mosque at Marrakesh.

Above right: A perspective of the outside aisle of multi-lobed arches supported on double columns at the Diwan-i-Am, or public audience hall, of the Red Fort at Delhi. Built by the Mogul emperor Shah Jehan, the masonry of the fort is carved from red sandstone.

and to the capitals and bases of the columns and piers. Similar treatment was also applied to arches over alcoves and other decorative features in wall surfaces. In the royal mosque at the Aljafería, the mihrab, the niche indicating the direction of Holy Mecca, is framed by a single horseshoe arch with alternate voussoirs carved with arabesques in relief. At the great mosque in Cordoba, the mihrab was aligned with the central arch of a triple archway built across the main space of the mosque. The view from the central bay of the prayer hall, looking towards the mihrab, is of three multi-lobed arches supported on carved capitals and marble columns. These are surmounted by a multi-lobed arcade, which is carried by the keystones of the lower arches. The upper arcade is interlaced with three horseshoe arches at the same level, supported on columns and capitals resting on the lower capitals. This complex archway is then topped by a single arch spanning the full width of the trio of arches. The complete upper structure is perforated by thirteen voids of varying sizes and patterns. Beyond this, another archway has three bays of interlacing multi-lobed arches surmounted by three simple horseshoe arches, again producing a perforated effect at the upper level. The horseshoe arch of the mihrab is visually framed by the lower central arch. The complete effect within the mosque was of a skilful pattern of solid, void, light and shade in three dimensions.

The manipulation of perforations in a modelled surface was also carried out, on a smaller scale, in the home. Because of the emphasis on family privacy in Islamic and some Christian societies, it was essential to prevent anyone from looking into the house from outside. However, it was also necessary that those inside should have a view of the outside world without being observed themselves. A device allowing one-way vision, as well as the

An interior view in the Alhambra, looking through a series of archways from the Hall of Two Sisters to a double-arched window in a mirador opening onto the enclosed garden of Daraxa. Here the entire decorative vocabulary of the Nasrid period is displayed.

A *jali*, or pierced marble screen, of such delicacy that it allows a clear view of the building opposite whilst maintaining internal privacy. This example is found in the mosque of Fatehpur Sikri, the city built by the Mogul emperor Akbar.

gardens; the whole garden was considered to be part of the zone of privacy and a continuous visual relationship between the external planted area and the interior of the pavilion was desired.

On a more modest domestic scale, there is another type of screen which is widely used in the Islamic world. This type is made from timber and is known as *mashrabiyya* in Arabic and *rowshan* in Persian. It consists of a timber framework containing an intricate grid of turned hardwood rods that fit together in an ingenious geometric pattern. These screens were normally fixed but sometimes incorporated small hinged shutters that opened within the larger panel. Such screens were usually set up around three sides of a projecting balcony window at the first or second storey of a private house. On the balcony was a raised platform on which long cushions were arranged. From here members of the household could observe, unseen and in comfort, the activities in the street below or the social life of the internal courtyard. The platform also had space for unglazed pottery jars. These contained water which was cooled by evaporation, and thus explain the origin of the word *mashrabiyya*, which is derived from the Arabic word for 'drink'.

A charming drawing in *The Coral Buildings of Suakin* by Jean-Pierre Greenlaw shows a woman peering out of a *rowshan* through an open top-hung shutter. Suakin was an important port on the Red Sea coast of Sudan. It is now in ruins but in the 1940s Greenlaw had the foresight to make a visual record of many of its houses before they deteriorated. Although the design of the houses shows influence from both Egypt and Turkey, the *rawashin* (plural of *rowshan*) were not made from turned timber elements as in Cairo but were composed of a latticework made up of members of small rectangular section. This type of lattice-

ingress of light and air, was needed; the solution was a form of perforated grille made from stone or plaster. Such grilles, known as *celosías* in Spain and *jalis* in India, were fixed in religious as well as domestic buildings wherever privacy was considered important. They were carved with great skill and precision and were based on geometric or floral patterns. An outstandingly beautiful example from India is the so-called Tree of Life grille found in the mosque built by Sidi Saiyid at Ahmadabad in the fifteenth century. The delicate stone tracery is composed of conventionalized vegetable forms with exquisite interlacing curves and is fine enough to rival the work of any Art Nouveau artist.

In hot climates these grilles had the additional advantage of allowing the entry of reflected light but of excluding direct sunlight, which would otherwise have heated interior surfaces and so increased the indoor temperature. In the pavilion in the gardens of the Generalife at the Alhambra, *celosías* were placed high up in the outer walls to provide ventilation and subdued lighting. At the lower level, openings allowed direct views into the

In direct sunlight the geometric patterns of the *jali* are reproduced in light and shade on the floor. This photograph from *Picturesque India* (1928) reveals the great variety of such patterns to be found in the windows of the tomb of Mohammed Ghaus in Gwalior, India. Built in the 1560s, this tomb is another example of immaculate Mogul craftsmanship.

John Frederick Lewis's oil painting of 1873, set in his own home in Cairo, shows a reception of female visitors to the harem. The *mashrabiyya* windows are painted with meticulous accuracy, showing the diffuse light from the lower turned wood sections compared with the more clearcut shadows of the coloured glass patterns set in the higher panels.

work was known as *shish* and such panels were often embellished with a variety of fretwork designs. The weight of the structure above these panels was usually carried by horizontal timber lintels so that the openings, where the panels were fitted, were simple rectangles. However, not all the decoration at Suakin was simple. Many of the houses had timber archways subdividing the internal space. These purely decorative elements were made from timber frames and panels shaped to resemble arches.

Some openings in Islamic buildings were filled with glass, which excludes air and rain while allowing the entry of light into the interior. Glazing dates from Roman times. It is probable that coloured glass was used before the technique of making plain transparent glass was discovered. Coloured glass was used in Byzantine churches and, later, was fixed in the windows of Ottoman mosques. Both plain transparent and coloured glass were fitted in the upper panels of *mashrabiyya* in the Mamlouk houses of Cairo. Various colours were arranged in a geometric pattern which echoed the decorative scheme of the turned rods in the lower panels. In his informative work *Manners and Customs of the Modern Egyptians*, which was published in 1836, E W Lane comments that: 'in the better houses of Cairo the windows of lattice work are now generally furnished with frames of glass on the inside, which in the winter are wholly closed; for a penetrating cold is felt in Egypt when the thermometer of Fahrenheit is below 60 degrees.' Having lived in Cairo for many years, Lane spoke from experience.

Spatially speaking, the walls are the most significant surfaces in a room, simply because they provide the most obvious and immediate definition of space. If that space is lofty and the lighting is bright, the eye is drawn upwards, or, conversely, downwards if the floor and its finish are colourful and feature strong contrasting patterns. If a room is well lit, it may also divert our attention from the vertical surfaces. If it gives access to another room or level, attention may also be focused on the floor or stairs.

Nevertheless, it is the walls and other vertical surfaces that mainly define a room or building and the dimensions of perceived space. Choice of material for the construction of the walls of Moorish buildings included stone of all kinds, burnt brick, concrete and, in some cases, earth (either beaten or in the form of sun-dried bricks). In some areas of the Islamic world, timber was incorporated to help hold the wall together and as a means of attaching timber windows and balconies. The area of plain wall influenced the choice of finish, colour and pattern. Large external areas of stone

or brickwork were usually treated with some form of patterning, using colour and texture, whereas internal wall surfaces were rarely left undecorated. Plaster, usually gypsum, was often applied to walls and decorated in patterns obtained by carving, moulding and painting. Other applied wall finishes included glazed and unglazed tiles and timber panelling. The latter was normally confined to internal or sheltered locations.

Islamic buildings are renowned for the delicate luxuriance of their surface decoration. Horizontal surfaces, like floors and ceilings, are treated in the same way. A typical example is the internal courtyard of the Bou Inania *madrassa* at Fez. The walls and pillars are faced with coloured glazed tiles arranged in a criss-cross geometric grid. Above the dado runs a horizontal frieze of Koranic calligraphic inscriptions, the glazed script contrasting with the unglazed background of tiles. Above the frieze, the wall is covered with elaborately carved stuccowork, and higher still are carved timber panels and lintels. Perforated timber screens stand

A similar balcony *mashrabiyya* window at first-floor level as drawn by Lewis from the courtyard below. This is one of the many drawings he made in the 1840s and shows an exterior typical of the larger Mamlouk houses in Cairo. Several of them have now been restored under the supervision of the Egyptian Government.

between the pillars up to dado level. The floor, the base of the central fountain and the drainage channels are paved with glazed tiles.

Before they pray, Muslims are required to perform ritual ablutions, including washing their feet. Before entering a place of worship, a palace or a residence, they remove their shoes to avoid spreading dirt from outside over the floor covering, which usually consists of woven carpets. Woven carpets have always been the most common internal floor covering in Muslim societies and it is the usual practice to squat on the carpet during religious discussions and instruction in the mosque, as well as at social gatherings. Raised platforms are used only by those considered to be of special importance, such as the scholar in the mosque, the ruler holding court in his palace and the head of the household in his reception room at home. Carpets vary in size and pattern, and prestige is attached to their size and quality. The carpets are richly patterned and the traditional use of natural dyes produces a subtly related range of hues. Woven fabrics are used only for floor coverings and not for wall decoration. Cushions, covered with woven fabric, are used for comfort.

Movable Western-style furniture was very rare. Low tables were used to carry metal trays for food and writing purposes but chairs were unknown until European influence was acknowledged by Muslim rulers and thus affected attitudes at their courts. To receive ambassadors and important dignitaries, the ruler, according to tradition, would sit against the centre of one wall, while his guests would squat in two parallel rows with their backs to the side walls. Those to whom precedence was given were seated nearest to the ruler. During the Mogul period in India, procedure for receiving important guests became much more formal and theatrical and could last for several days. It was known as a *durbar* and its practice was adopted by the British, especially towards the closing stages of the imperial era.

The choice of finish for ceilings was limited by the type of structure supporting the floor or roof above the enclosed space. The area and the distance between the walls would have determined the structural system. If the area was relatively modest, horizontal timber beams were usually selected to take the load. The beams could be arranged along one or two axes and, because their depth gave them strength and rigidity, they would normally project below the surface of the ceiling and so divide it into rectangular bays or panels. This ceiling treatment was normal in domestic architecture and was also commonly adopted in palaces. The three faces of the projecting beam were often carved and painted. The *artesonado* ceiling was a feature of Spanish Mudéjar buildings and often used in the construction of churches.

In 1492 a throne room was constructed for King Ferdinand and Queen Isabella inside the palace of the Aljaferìa at Saragossa. It is an impressive room, high in proportion to its ground

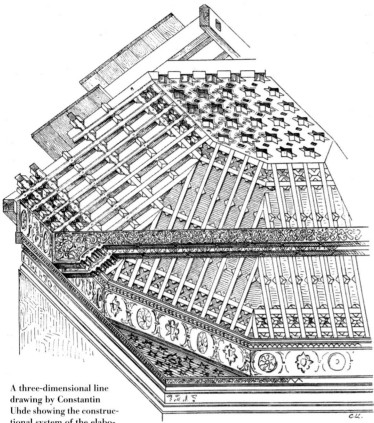

A three-dimensional line drawing by Constantin Uhde showing the constructional system of the elaborate timber roof and ceiling in the church of San Il Defonso at Alcala de Henares in Castile. The timber truss and its exposed tie beams are clearly shown, as well as the decorated timbers of the sloping and horizontal surfaces of the ceiling. This is a typical example of the *artesonado* work of Mudéjar carpenters.

surfaces. To complete the effect of royal splendour, an arcaded gallery for guests runs around all four walls below the *artesonado* ceiling. Below the gallery is a richly embellished cornice incorporating a calligraphic inscription in Latin praising the Catholic monarchs, their victory and the liberation of Andalusia from the Moors in 1492. There is a certain irony in this since the first moves to create a new royal palace in the Aljafería were made under the supervision of a Mudéjar, Faraig de Gali, in 1488, just two years after the headquarters of the Holy Inquisition in Aragon had been established in the palace itself. De Gali continued to supervise the works after 1492 and when he died in 1508 his son, Mahoma de Gali, succeeded him, with the agreement of the officials of the Inquisition.

As described in Chapter Two, the problem of relating a dome to a square base was solved by an elaborate architectural feature known in Arabic as a *muqarna*, which achieves the transition from circle to square through a niche related to the stalactite. What had originally been used singly and on a relatively large scale was later developed on a smaller scale; the *muqarna* was repeated and used in groups because of its capacity to create a decorative texture. It lost its structural function and was carved from stucco, which was often supported on a special timber framework. It was widely used as a purely decorative feature for ceilings and soffits, arches, vaults and domes. It was repeated incessantly like a honeycomb, brilliantly painted and gilded. The resultant impression of luxury is unique and overwhelming, an effect that has not always found favour with Western scholars. For example, Sir Banister Fletcher, in his *History of Architecture on the Comparative Method* (1945 edition), refers to the Alhambra, where the *muqarna* is used in many areas for surface deco-

area and well-suited to important ceremonial occasions. It has a magnificent *artesonado* ceiling with beams that span in two directions to form coffers on a square grid. Each coffer has an octagonal inset with a carved and gilt pine cone at its centre. According to local legend, the gold used in this room was the first to be brought back from the New World. The undersides of the beams are decorated with interlacing geometric patterns with octagonal stars at their intersections. The throne room and the adjoining apartments have a sumptuous character thanks to the generous use of gilding and primary colours on walls and ceilings. Ceramic tiles in brightly coloured geometric patterns decorate the floors and lower wall

Opposite: The magnificent gilded timber *artesonado* ceiling and gallery to the throne room at the Aljafería palace at Saragossa. The date of its construction, 1492, can be seen at the right-hand corner of the continuous Latin inscription which runs along the base of the projecting gallery.

Above: The ceiling of myriad *muqarnas* to the dome over the Hall of the Abencerrages, which opens off the Court of Lions at the Alhambra. Its plan is based on the eight-pointed star and in the drum there are sixteen clerestory windows which allow the sun at daybreak and sunset to fall on the intersecting planes, creating a kaleidoscopic effect of golden light.

Right: Two line drawings from Owen Jones and Jules Goury, illustrating a section through an octagonal dome above the Hall of Two Sisters in the Alhambra.

ration, as being in the Spanish Saracenic style. Though he describes it as a 'gorgeous pleasure palace', he goes on to say that 'here a surfeit of surface decoration, easily carried out in plaster and colour, takes the place of a more monumental treatment, and suited the fatalistic nature of people who were content to build for the present rather than for all time'.

The dome features prominently in Persian architecture, where it has a greater vertical dimension. This makes it appear tall and pointed from the outside, particularly in large-scale religious buildings. By decorating the curved surfaces with the same patterned finish as the vertical surfaces, the Persians gave their mosques a wonderfully rich unity. A superb example of diversity within this unity is the design of the mosque of Sheikh Lutfullah at Isfahan. The view of this mosque from the Meidan is dominated by the pointed outline of the dome rising slightly off-centre above the entrance portal, or *iwan*. The dome is set on a circular drum in which the dominant colour is blue-green and which incorporates a number of perforated arched openings that admit light to the interior. The junction of dome and drum is emphasized by a band of calligraphy on a blue background. In contrast, the background colour of the dome is buff brick, overlaid with an extremely complex pattern of arabesques outlined in black, white and blue. Blue is also used to highlight certain points of emphasis and to pick out the apex, which is crowned by three spheres, a religious symbol. The predominantly blue *iwan* is faced with ceramic tiles in many different floral patterns. The entrance door is centrally placed, below a large recessed pointed arch whose soffit is decorated with elaborate *muqarnas*. Below the *muqarnas* and above the door is another band of calligraphy with light cursive script on a dark background. This magnificent opening leads into a dim vaulted corridor, which runs along two sides of the square prayer space until it reaches the entrance opposite the mihrab, an indirect approach made necessary by the conflict between the north-south orientation of the Meidan and the direction of Holy Mecca.

The interior of this mosque is as majestic as the exterior. It is lit by bluish reflected light entering through the tiled grille

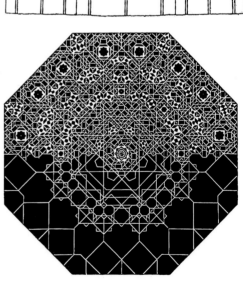

This coloured lithograph, dating from 1853, is by Baron Isidore Taylor. It depicts the Hall of the Abencerrages at the Alhambra, clearly delineating the geometry of the *muquarnas*.

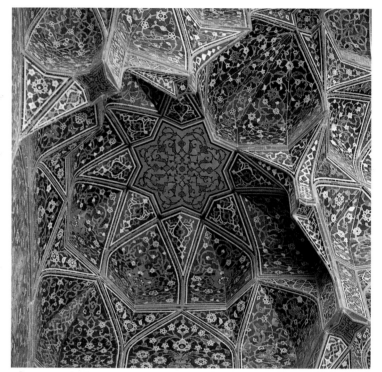

Right: Close-up of the dome of the Mosque of Lutfullah in Isfahan. The prominent shape of the dome rises above the main portal of the mosque, which faces directly onto the Meidan. The golden brown of the dome's bricks, with their inset ceramic arabesque patterns, contrasts with the predominant turquoise and blue of the calligraphy and the windows of the drum.

Far right: Detail of some ceramic *muqarnas* at the Mosque of the Shah at Isfahan. The irregularly shaped tiles incorporate a flat eight-pointed star.

windows in the drum. The transition from the square ground plan to the circular plan of the dome above is achieved by the use of an intervening octagon formed by eight great arches, four in the side walls and four in the form of niches. Their inner surfaces are richly decorated with turquoise tilework in a cable pattern. A sunburst of arabesque tracery in the centre of the dome descends to form a pattern of lozenges arranged in a lattice of brick and tile which increase in size as they move downwards. Two bands of calligraphy, one above and one below the arched grilles, decorate the drum. The remaining solid surfaces of the drum and the squinches are finished with an intricate arabesque tracery of polychrome glazed tiles. The setting-out of both the internal and external tilework in complex patterns on curved surfaces demonstrates a knowledge of applied

geometry that has probably never been equalled in architecture before or since. The external space of the Meidan and the interior of the mosque are separate; there is no possibility of seeing the one from the other. The dim corridor is the link between them and provides an opportunity to pause and prepare the mind for prayer. By definition the interior of a mosque is an inward-looking space where no outside distraction is permitted.

The throne room at the Alhambra, however, commands a direct view without, so that a relationship exists between the internal and the external space. This was often the intention of the designers of Islamic palaces, *madrassas* and houses. However, the external space was usually enclosed, forming a courtyard or patio which did not open to the street or any public space and thus ensured privacy and security. Visual links between the rooms

Close-up of part of the main entrance portal of the Mosque of the Shah, facing the Meidan. This view looks up towards the curved recess and stalactite construction above another niche in the centre. All of this is just below the gigantic pointed archway of the portal.

and courtyard were encouraged so long as the distinction between guest and family zones was maintained. The sound of fountains and the charm of flowers and shrubs were balm to a people for whom the harshness of the desert was an all-too-familiar environment. It is not surprising, therefore, that the Muslim vision of Paradise is a garden with water, fountains, shady trees and luxuriant vegeta-tion, the very antithesis of the desert, where water is more valuable than gold. Islam did not actually originate in the desert but in Mecca, a trading city on the edge of the desert, where Bedouin came to trade. So for many Muslims life became a symbolic journey through the desert in search of an oasis or paradise which was in actuality attainable only after death.

Above: A ground-floor reception room in a Cairo house, as illustrated by Prisse d'Avennes in his *L'Art Arabe d'après les monuments du Kaire* (1869–77). Known as a '*mandar'ah*' and intended for male guests, this room has a lowered central section called a '*durka'ah*' which contains a fountain. Visitors would take their shoes off before moving to the upper level.

Right: A sketch of such a fountain in E W Lane's *Manners and Customs of the Modern Egyptians*, his account of life in Cairo published in 1836. The pool is decorated with black and white marble inlaid with fine red tiles.

For the Arabs the presence of water cannot be taken for granted, its sources being few and far between. Besides great rivers, water might be found in springs, at oases, and in fertile areas to which it was brought by man-made irrigation through canals and ditches. Gardens were conceived as idealized forms of irrigation and were formally divided into quarters, symbolizing the four rivers of life. Again, geometry was used to develop an exercise in pattern-making. Still water became a means of reflecting buildings, trees, plants and shrubs, adding to the splendour of the built environment. The joys of flowing water, inspired by the charms of natural springs, were then introduced artificially into garden design. Where possible, changes of level were made to create cascades and an increasing knowledge of the science of hydraulics led to the development of more ingenious fountains. This not only made possible more plant life but also cooled the micro-climate by evaporation. This principle was clearly understood by the builders of the Mamlouk courtyard houses of Cairo. The central part of the ground-floor reception room was paved with marble and accommodated a fountain at its mid-point.

The Generalife, literally the 'garden of the architect', is sited outside the main palace area of the Alhambra but within its fortified walls. Above the garden stands the summer villa of the Nasrid dynasty, which reputedly was bought from one of the architects of the Alhambra. Two main pavilions are

linked by an enclosed rectangular court which embraces a long marble-lined water channel. At either end of the channel is a jet fountain set in a circular basin. The channel continues in a loop, reaching other enclosures adorned with pools, shady trees and vegetation. When Théophile Gautier visited the Alhambra in 1842, a huge oleander (rose laurel) stood at the centre of one of these ponds. So moved was he by its incomparable beauty that he wrote a poem entitled *Dans le Generalife il est un laurier-rose*.

> There's a rose laurel in the Generalife
> That shines like love or victory in full cry –
> Its nurse (a fountain) tenders it relief
> In a shower of pearls o'er flower and leaf
> Whose cool lustre disdains the fiery sky.

The garden also contains many cypresses and numerous box hedges and roses. A hilltop mirador, reached by several flights of steps with channels of running water at handrail height, stands high above the summer villa. The steps are punctuated with jet fountains at different levels and the landings are surrounded by shade-giving trees from which magnificent vistas of the Alhambra and views of the city below can be enjoyed. Beyond stretches the Vega, the plain celebrated by the poet Lorca, and above rise the snowcapped peaks of the Sierra Nevada, contrasting with the sugar-cane plantations and the palm trees below.

The celebrated medieval scholar Ibn Khaldoun visited Granada and later wrote a monumental history of the world. In the introduction, which he called the *Muqaddimah* and which is a major work

Above left: The fountain in the garden of Daraxa, as seen through the window in the mirador of Daraxa which opens off the Hall of Two Sisters at the Alhambra.

Above right: The Generalife, the summer villa of the Nasrids, is situated in the grounds, but outside the walls, of the Alhambra. It is surrounded by vegetation and has a long formal enclosed garden with a narrow pool, punctuated by fountains, running along its centre.

Right: A formal garden laid out with planting, pools and fountains at Tippu's summer palace in Mysore, India.

Far right: A miniature by Bishan Das and Nanha from the manuscript of the Baburnama, or memoirs of Babur, which was commissioned by Akbar. Babur, the founder of the Mogul dynasty, is laying out the Garden of Fidelity or Bagh-i-wafa. This garden is believed to be near Jelalabad in Afghanistan, where the remains of a Mogul garden have been found.

in itself, he discussed at length the relationship between man's physical environment and social organization. For this he has been called the 'Father of Sociology'. In the section dealing with architecture, which he considered the first and oldest of the crafts, he stressed the need to protect the occupants of a building from the extremes of heat and cold. Possibly because he lost both his parents in the plague in Tunis, he believed bad air to be a cause of disease and insisted on the need for ventilation, cleanliness and flowing water.

Another garden, on a larger scale but equally celebrated by poets and lovers of the exotic, is the Shalamar (Abode of Love) at Lahore. This garden in the Persian tradition was created three centuries after on the orders of the Mogul emperor Shah Jehan, builder of the Taj Mahal. This legendary garden was designed by Ali Mardan Khan who was also responsible for the Shalamar garden at Kashmir which was made for Jahangir, Shah Jehan's father. In order to make the garden possible, a canal was constructed to bring the waters of the river Ravi to the chosen site. Nine years later, in 1642, the Shalamar was complete and ready for the emperor's opening visit. It was laid out on a grand scale with pools and fountains, a bath house and several pavilions. There are three terraces: the middle level contains the great reservoir, which is over sixty metres wide and is said to have contained no less than 152 fountains. In the centre stood a marble platform and a white marble throne, where the emperor could sit directly over the water. From here he could watch the fountains by moonlight, listening to the murmuring of the water and enjoying the scent of the exotic plants. Among these plants were probably fruit trees like

Left: A view of the gardens and hedges around the Generalife, the summer villa outside the walls of the Alhambra, Granada.

upwards so that they faced the cascades and so that new delights were gradually revealed until the highest and most private level (*zenana*) was attained. There is a difference in level of about five metres between the entrance and the *zenana* at Lahore.

The buildings surrounding the Shalamar garden at Lahore were of intricate design and faultless workmanship. (Unfortunately, in the eighteenth century, they were stripped of their marble and agate by Sikh craftsmen who used them to decorate buildings at Amritsar.) There were four main pavilions on the higher terrace and another four at the reservoir level. At the lowest level, facing down the main axis, was the hall of audience and, because the garden and associated buildings were used to accommodate the imperial court whenever it visited Lahore, there was also a bath suite, or *hammam*.

The requirement of ablution before prayer emphasizes the importance placed on cleanliness in Muslim society. The *hammam* was, therefore, an essential element in urban design. Each residential quarter had at least two bath houses, one for men and one for women. Each palace was provided with its own facilities and these followed the principles first adopted by the Romans and later used in Western countries in the form of what was referred to as a Turkish bath. The *hammam*, in some form or other, is found throughout the Islamic world and

mango, cherry, apricot, peach, plum, apple, quince, lemon and orange, as well as fragrant flowers such as jasmine, rose, oleander and pandanus, while aspen and plane trees were planted for shade. It was customary for visitors to enter Mogul gardens at the lowest level and to progress

The interior of a barber's shop in the French quarter of Cairo, as depicted in *The Architecture of Arabia and the Monuments of Cairo* (1829) by Pascal Xavier Coste.

layout usually comprised a changing area leading to the bathing area, which included a hot room (*calidarium*) immediately next to the furnace and a cooler space (*tepidarium*). Both hot water and hot air were circulated, the latter through ducts in the floor in the manner of the Roman hypocaust. After bathing and massage, rest and relaxation took place in a room set aside for the purpose.

In the royal bath house at the Alhambra, as well as a bath reserved for the use of the queen, there is a lofty saloon where the royal family could relax on luxurious carpets and cushions around a central fountain, listening to the royal musicians playing in the gallery above. This practice did not cease after the Christian Reconquest. Ferdinand and Isabella stayed in the palace on many occasions, and Charles V, the Holy Roman Emperor, used the large-scale palace in Renaissance style that he built alongside only for state occasions. He spent his honeymoon in the Alhambra and renovated the baths with new glazed tiling. Philip V, the first of the Bourbon kings of Spain, visited the Alhambra with his queen in 1730. This was the scene that Manuel de Falla, when writing the music to accompany the poem *Psyche* by the French poet G Jean Aubry, visualized, as he invoked the kind of concert that might have taken place during that visit in the Queen's boudoir at the top of one of the high towers, from which there is a magnificent view. The composer tried to capture the scene of the Queen's ladies singing and dancing the mythological story of Psyche and Cupid.

James Cavanagh Murphy, who visited the Alhambra in 1802, was so impressed with the baths that he measured them in great detail. His drawings clearly show the construction and the layout of the various rooms. The concert room has a gallery on the first floor and a raised lantern above with grille windows which shed diffused light

its use has become a ritual lasting several hours. Bathing in hot and cold water was often combined with massage. As well as washing the body, bathing involved specified periods in the steam room and the cool waiting room for reasons of health and cures prescribed by physicians. In a palace or large house, the *hammam* would naturally be situated in the private family zone and would have no windows in the outside walls. The

This miniature in the Persian style by the master Bihzad of Herat, dated 1494, shows the Caliph Mamoun in a Turkish bath. It is an illustration from the manuscript of the *Khamsa* or five poems by Nizami.

This engraving from James Murphy's *Arabian Antiquities of Spain* (1813–16) shows the King's bath in the Alhambra. The vaulted roof is pierced with star-patterned ventilators which admit a soft light.

on to the space below. The bath houses, on the other hand, are single-storeyed, with vaulted roofs pierced with star-shaped holes for light and ventilation. This type of construction had been standard for bath houses since the eighth century, as the baths in the palace at Qasr Amra in Jordan demonstrate. Here the inside surfaces of the vault were painted blue so that the ventilation holes suggested stars in the night sky.

At the Alhambra, the walls of the bath house were brightly decorated to prevent a claustrophobic effect. Every surface is covered with carved timber and plaster at the higher levels. The columns and capitals are of white marble, as is the floor, which is inset with panels of patterned tiles. In order to make cleaning easier and to minimize damage from water and steam, the finishes in the bath rooms are simpler and more functional. The walls are lined with glazed tiles in multicoloured geometric patterns up to head height, with a frieze of tiles in arabesque patterns above. Both the floors and the large rectangular basins are lined with slabs of white marble. These smooth, reflecting surfaces are brought to sparkling life by light passing through the star-shaped perforations, which are lined with green glazing. The decoration in the concert room is the most intricate, with patterned glazed tiles at dado level.

A favoured visiting dignitary might have been invited to enjoy the intimate spaces of the royal bath house. After a bath and a massage, relaxing on the cushions in the concert room and listening to the musicians, he might well have pondered the complexity of the surrounding colours and patterns and its parallel in the poetry and music of the court.

The two-storeyed concert room in the suite of baths at the Alhambra as depicted by Murphy (left). The musicians would have played in the gallery above while the royal family relaxed in luxury after their ablutions (below). It is likely that after the Reconquest Charles V and other Christian monarchs used these facilities.

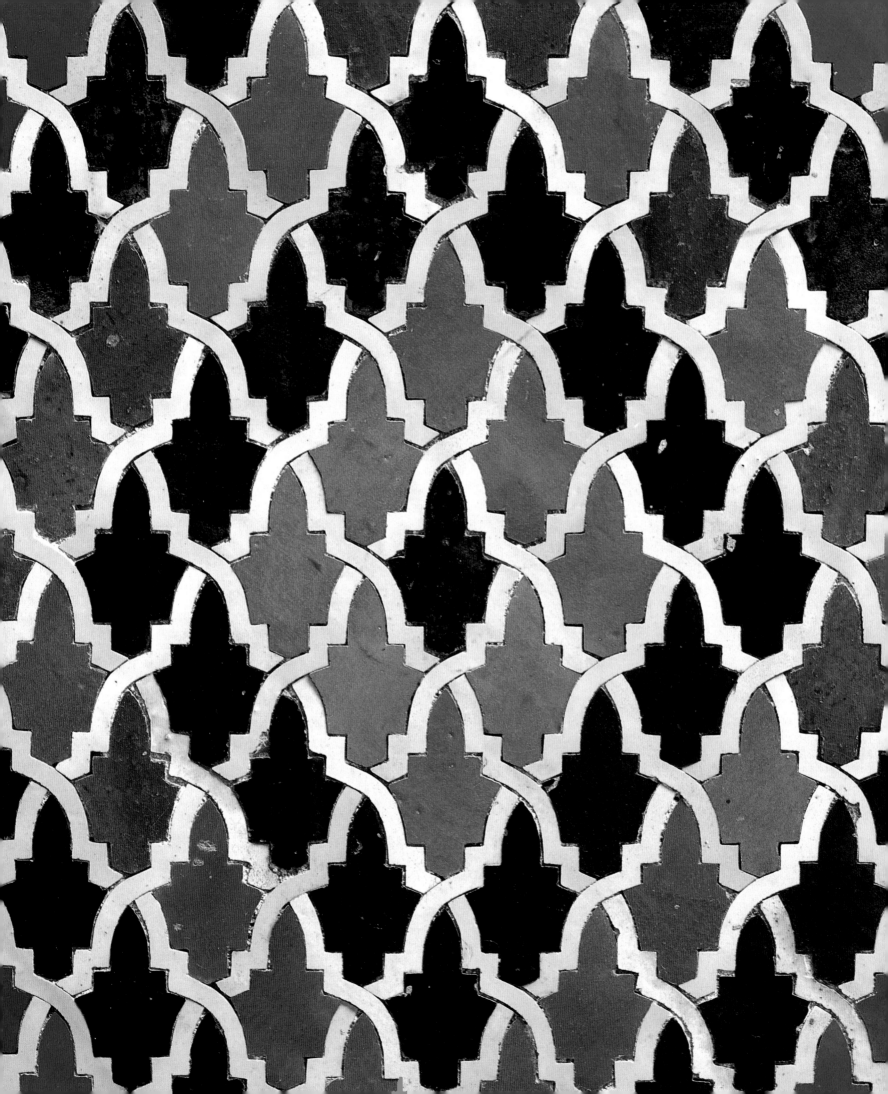

Opposite: Glazed ceramic tiles typical of Moorish design in their pattern and colours – turquoise, terracotta, blue, black and white.

Right: A tympanum from the Great Mosque of Qous illustrated in Volume II of *L'Art Arabe* (1869–77) by Prisse d'Avennes. The arabesques are skilfully related to the space contained by the form of the pointed arch and the horizontal base.

One can say of it that it is a second Paradise in this respect,
That whoever leaves this garden is filled with regret.
Abu Talib Kalim

The 'Tree of Life' *jali* in the mosque of Sidi Sayyid at Ahmadabad, dating from 1572, represents a peak in stone carving skills in Islamic India. The use of sinuous curves was probably inspired by Hindu sculpture. This *jali* may also have influenced artists and craftsmen of the Art Nouveau period as it was a popular subject for Victorian photographers.

The transformation of plain surfaces by means of decoration, thereby making those surfaces more attractive, and architecturally more significant, is an inherent characteristic of Moorish style. The predominant methods of such decoration are the use of abstract patterns, calligraphy and colour. Each has its own significance.

Patterns most typical of Moorish are those that have flowing outlines and that incorporate lines and shapes in different combinations. These flowing shapes are normally called 'arabesques', a name ascribed by Westerners to decorative patterns of Eastern origin. They were generally derived from shapes observed in nature and can usually be traced back to stylized plant forms. The inspiration came mainly from plants that have undulating reverse curves. In *The Grammar of Ornament*, writing on the category of decoration he termed 'Moresque', Owen Jones stated that all lines grow out of each other in gradual undulations and that

all transitions of curved lines from curved or straight lines must be gradual in order to obtain the repose necessary to achieve true beauty. He went on to cite the analogy of the vine leaf and its need to distribute the sap from the parent stem to the extremities. In this way every ornament can be traced back to its branch and root. Using the image of interlacing leaves and branches winding back on themselves, he demonstrated the principles of radiation from a parent stem, continuity of line and tangential curvature.

Such natural patterns are found in the ornamentation of the Alhambra in Granada and of the mihrab of the Great Mosque in Damascus. Other plant forms – for example, the acanthus, the palm, the pomegranate, the cypress and a wide variety of flowers – are also used. In the representation of natural plant forms, line and rhythm are vital. Although these patterns are by their very nature fixed in time and space, their visual rhythm

A selection of arabesque motifs from the ornamentation of the Alhambra and the Great Mosque at Cordoba. These drawings are by Constantin Uhde and appear in his book *Monuments in Spain and Portugal*, published in Berlin in 1892.

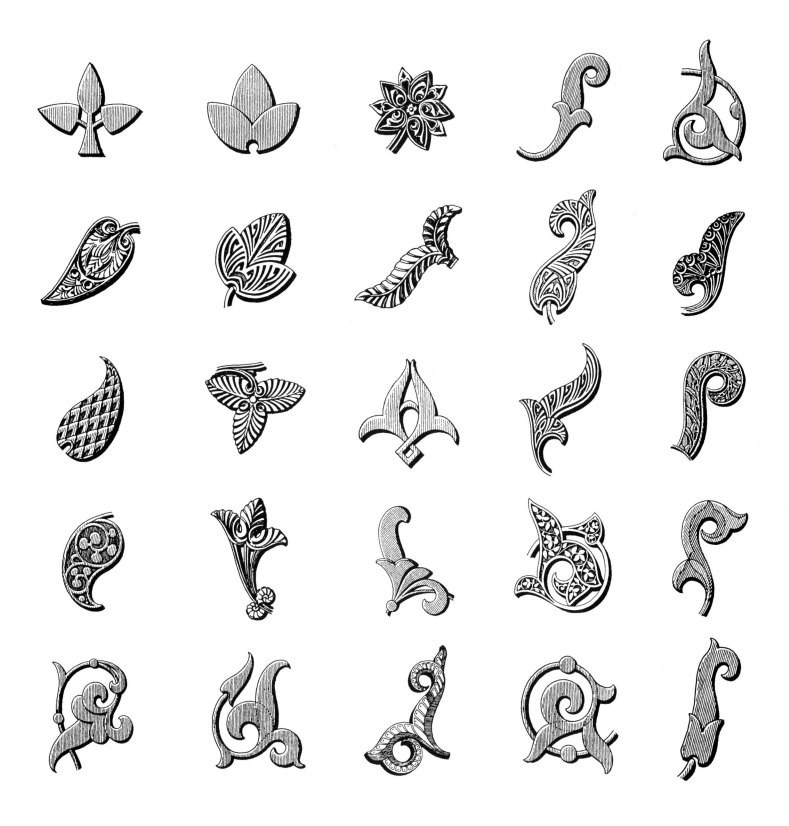

Twelve examples of the designs from the Alhambra which Owen Jones termed 'Moresque Ornament' and which appeared in his *Grammar of Ornament* (1856). He referred to their basic patterns as lozenge diapers and went on to state that 'composed of but three colours, they are more harmonious and effective than any others in our collection, and possess a peculiar charm which all the others fail to approach'.

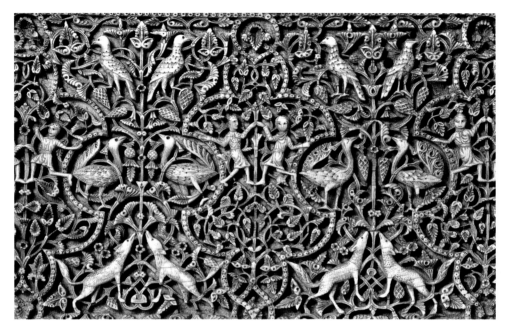

suggests movement and thus time. In its submission to the wind, a cypress displays undulating reverse curves that result from a chain of events through time. These curves, according to Sufi doctrine, suggest the masculine and feminine principle in a similar way to the Chinese symbol of Ying and Yang.

Interlacing is a common and important characteristic of the arabesque. The arabesque may be absolutely flat, as it is on a glazed ceramic tile, or in relief, if it is carved in timber, stone or stucco. It may also involve the solid and the void. It often occurs in window grilles, when it is carved in a flowing linear interlacing 'Tree of Life' pattern, as in the exquisite window grille (*jali*) in the Sidi Sayyid mosque at Ahmadabad. In this example, a third dimension is suggested by the slight raising of the stone surface of one branch as it passes in front of another but the total effect of the pattern remains two-dimensional. The palmette, a stylized version of the palm leaf, is another motif that

appears either in a simple symmetrical form or combined with flowing interlacing stems to create intricate decorative patterns.

Probably the best-known stylized motif based on a natural form is the paisley pattern. This was first introduced to Britain as the main decorative motif on woven silk shawls imported from Kashmir in the late eighteenth century. When the Napoleonic wars interfered with maritime trade with India, these very popular shawls soon became scarce and expensive. It was then economically advantageous to produce similar shawls in Britain, and the Scottish town of Paisley became the dominant centre for this type of textile production. The paisley pattern has since been used in an infinite variety of forms in both woven and printed fabrics of all kinds, as well as on printed wallpapers. Its source, which is ancient, possibly dating back to Babylonian times, is not clear. Valerie Reilly states that it is thought to represent the tightly curled palm frond just as it begins to grow. In Persia the

A carved ivory panel from a casket of the early eleventh century, the Caliphal period of Islamic Spain. There are stones and traces of pigment in the floral arabesque patterns which are merged with bird, animal and human images.

Right: A fabric design
by George Haité for
paisley shawls, dated 1871.
The form of the design
is said to derive from
the '*buteh*' pattern used
in Kashmir shawls.

Bottom left: An original
'*buteh*' or shrub pattern
incorporated in the design
of an eighteenth-century
shawl from Kashmir.

Bottom right: Another
fabric design by George
Haité for paisley shawls.

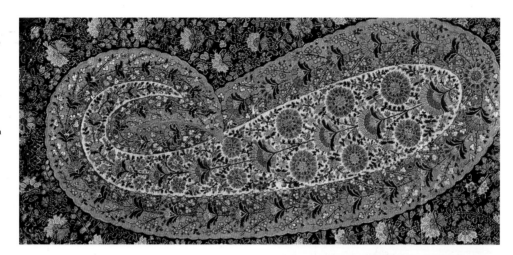

motif was called '*buteh*', meaning shrub, and in India it is currently referred to as the mango pattern. Whatever its origins, it is unique and instantly recognizable.

Arabesques of all types are frequently used by potters today as hand-painted decoration on the flowing plastic surfaces of vessels, containers and lamps. They are also used in the same way to decorate metal and glassware. This form of decoration was commonplace in Islamic countries and was then adopted in Europe, frequently appearing on articles produced by Muslim craftsmen working in the West. Many Muslims settled in Venice, and metalwork in a style often referred to as Venetian Saracenic resulted. Some beautiful examples of ivory carved with arabesques survive from Islamic Spain at the time of the Caliphate. A combination of arabesque patterns and stylized human and animal figures, illustrating hunting scenes and the pleasures of courtly life also appear on ivory plaques thought to originate in early twelfth-century Egypt. Islam allowed human and animal figures

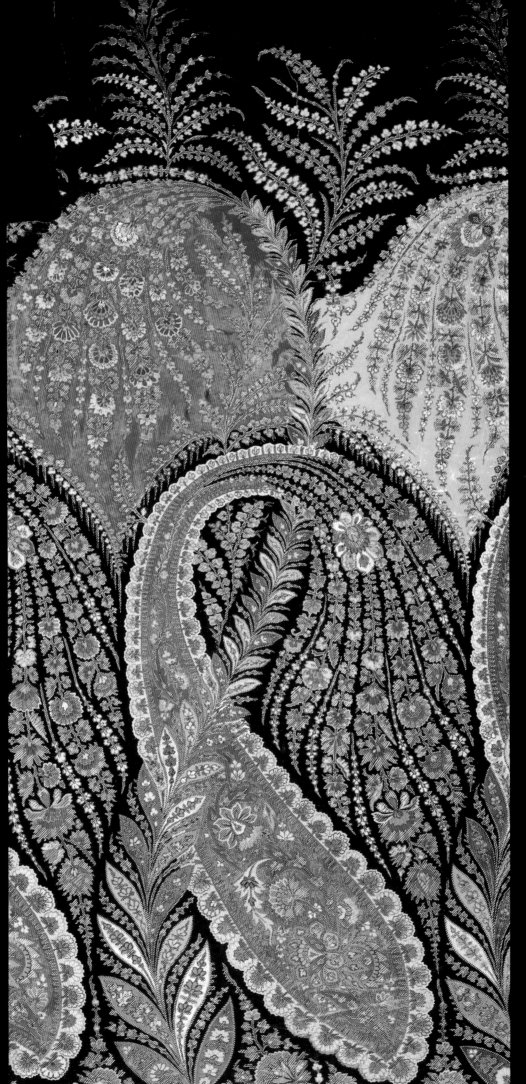

A design by George
Haité in watercolour and
gouache for a printed
paisley shawl. It is an elegant and colourful com-
position combining
developed versions of the
'*buteh*' form with interlacing arabesques and elabo-
rate floral patterns.
Haité was an artist and
designer who lived from
1825 to 1871.

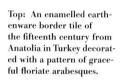

Top: An enamelled earthenware border tile of the fifteenth century from Anatolia in Turkey decorated with a pattern of graceful floriate arabesques.

Centre: An arabesque design with a peony motif from a Persian manuscript of the *Khamsa* by Nizami.

Bottom: A floral arabesque border to a carpet of the Safavid period, the classic age of the Persian carpet. This example is in wool pile on cotton.

to appear in the domestic environment but excluded them from all religious contexts. In architecture, the curved exterior surface of a stone-faced dome was often covered with a decorative net of interlacing floral arabesques and geometric patterns. Several examples from the Mamlouk period are on view in Cairo.

The most widespread use of the arabesque, however, was as decoration for flat surfaces. Ceramic tiles were often painted with an underglaze pattern of coloured arabesques. These tiles were used to face walls, often at dado level, and on rare occasions on floors. The most striking use of the arabesque at floor level was in the interlacing forms which appeared on carpets and prayer mats, which demonstrate the skills of weavers in creating rhythmic lines and rich colour contrasts. In Koranic manuscripts and leather bindings, the arabesque combined with calligraphy resulted in works of intricate beauty that clearly convey a sense of reverential joy.

Interlacing was frequently applied to the fluidity of the arabesque's reverse curves. It also features in the infinite number of ways in which geometric patterns can be created with straight lines. Geometric interlacing in the form of a knot or braid is frequently used in borders. Geometric patterning is based on a repeat unit which is usually set out in a drawing based on a circle. For the Muslim craftsman the setting-out process is a satisfying activity in that geometry is a direct expression of divine unity, within which there is limitless diversity. Geometry, which depends on an understanding of numbers, was developed in ancient Mesopotamian and Egyptian times for measuring land and making astronomical calculations. The Greeks, and Euclid in particular, extended this knowledge and thus formed the starting-point for Islamic mathematics. The Indians and Persians also contributed to the

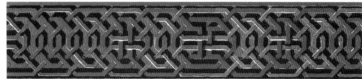

development of mathematics. The Arabs used numbers both in a practical manner and as the basis for a symbolic view of the cosmos. Arabic numerals, which reached the West in the tenth century, gradually replaced Roman numerals because, by introducing the concept of zero, they made tabular calculation the norm and thus rendered the abacus redundant. Although Arabic numerals have since become almost universal, they are not used in the majority of Arabic-speaking countries, where another form of notation, called 'Indian', is used. The decimal system and the mathematical discipline now known as algebra, which was fully established in the Islamic world, also reached the West during the tenth century. By then geometry had become the basis of harmony and discipline in Islamic visual art and numerical symbolism the essence of poetry and music.

El Said and Parman have explained the underlying principle of Islamic geometric patterning as a system whereby geometrical grids form the framework of identical units that are regularly repeated. They argue that a simple approach was used for

Three geometric continuous line border patterns, two of which are interlacing. The top two are from Volume I of *L'Art Arabe d'après les monuments du Kaire* (1869–77) by Prisse d'Avennes while the bottom one is from Volume II of Owen Jones and Jules Goury's *Plans, Elevations, Sections and Details of the Alhambra*, published in 1845.

Right: Geometrical setting-out of a repeat unit based on a hexagon within a circle and a repeat pattern derived from it, as demonstrated by Issam El-Said and Ayse Parman in *Geometrical Concepts in Islamic Art* (1976).

Far right: The same pattern with a hexagonal star inserted within it. This is a plate from Owen Jones and Jules Goury's study of the Alhambra.

solving the problem of setting out a grid. A length of rope could be divided into any number of parts using any convenient unit of measurement, such as the hand, arm, foot or stride. The required number of units could then be obtained by folding the given length into two, three or five equal pieces. Further units could be obtained by folding these units in half and thereby doubling the number produced by the previous fold. This technique, which depends only on whole numbers and avoids fractions, is still used in some parts of Asia and Africa. Another traditional technique in current use involves the compass and ruler. Any regular polygon can be generated from a circle if the circumference is divided equally into the required number of sections and straight lines are drawn joined between the points of division. The equilateral triangle, the square, pentagon, hexagon, octagon, and so on, can all be drawn by this method.

Repeat units are obtained by different methods. The surface to be decorated is divided into an equal number of parts. The number of these parts is equal to the total number of repeat units required. The entire area is then covered with circles whose diameters are equal to the subdivisions. By drawing a square around each circle, a grid of squares is then obtained, each square thus becoming a repeat unit. If straight lines are drawn to join the centre points of each side of this

Far left: An alcove in the Court of the Myrtles at the Alhambra. The tiled dado is decorated with a pattern similar to that drawn by Jones and Goury on the opposite page.

Top left: Geometrical setting-out of a repeat unit based on a square and an octagon within a circle. The repeat pattern derived from it incorporates an octagonal star at the centre. This drawing is also by Issam El-Said and Ayse Parman.

Bottom left: The above pattern used as incised ornament at the Alhambra.

square, another smaller square is obtained within it. The area of the smaller square is half that of the larger and the proportion of the side of the circumscribed square to the side of the inscribed square is 1 to the square root of 2. This process can be continued by inscribing progressively smaller squares in the same way. Thus the sides of the squares are progressively halved if only the

squares with vertical and horizontal sides are considered. If the diagonals of the first square are drawn and if lines are drawn to join the intersections with the original circle, another square is created. The area of this square is equal to that of the original inscribed square and the two together form an octagonal star. By continuing this process of point-joining, another system of subdivision is initiated. The repeat unit of the design could be applied practically by means of a full-scale template with holes pierced at the intersections of the grid lines. This system was used in the setting-out of mosaics and for the structural components and decorative patterns of lattice woodwork. The sys-

Above: This carved stone grille, based on the setting-out of the hexagonal repeat units but expressed in a linear interlacing pattern centred on hexagonal stars, is from the Selimiye Mosque at Edirne.

Right: A variety of geometrical repeat patterns derived from the square and the hexagon, as used in Moorish ornamentation. The example at the top right incorporates curves. At the middle of the third column there is a twelve-pointed star at the centre of a hexagon, while at the bottom right there is a similar star within a super-imposed octagon. Interlacing occurs in the top left and top right examples.

tem of proportioning based on the square and the octagonal star has an infinite variety of possibilities. When used on floors, the patterns can easily be integrated with spaces that are square or octagonal in plan, and can ensure a co-ordinated juncture between floor and walls.

A second system of proportion, one based on the hexagonal star, can be used to create geometric patterns. Using compasses the area to be decorated is divided into the number of parts equal to the number of times the repeat unit is to be incorporated into the design. The repeat unit, a hexagon inscribed within a circle, is obtained by using the circle's radius to divide its circumference into six equal arcs. The intersections are then joined by straight lines. The grid is formed by drawing hexagonal stars within each hexagon. These stars are formed either by joining the alternate corners of the hexagon or the alternate midpoints of the sides. The hexagonal star can also be seen as two overlapping equilateral triangles. The hexagon can similarly be made up of six equilateral triangles, their bases formed by the sides of the hexagon while the other two sides are the radii of the containing circle. The hexagon and the equilateral tri-

angle are thus seen to be closely related. The hexagonal star system can be developed by progressively dividing the diameter of the circle in the ratio of 1:2. A regular hexagon contains a rectangle which can be drawn in three positions and whose diagonals intersect at the centre of the containing circle. If the short side of this rectangle is taken to be 1, then the diagonal is root 3. As with the square, an infinite variety of patterns can be developed from the hexagonal star and the equilateral triangles that it contains.

Another variation is the double hexagon, which can be drawn by dividing the circumference of the circle into 12 equal parts. By joining alternate points in the circle's circumference, two hexagons are then inscribed within it. The repeat unit can then be one of the inscribed hexagons or the circumscribed square. Yet another extensive range of patterns can be established and under this system both the root 2 and root 3 methods of proportioning are combined. The patterns produced in this way include equilateral triangles, squares, hexagons, octagons, dodecagons and their stars. Probably the most sophisticated range of visual geometric harmonies is thereby created.

Yet another range of geometric patterns can be developed by using the five-sided figure, or pentagon. To construct a pentagon it is necessary to take a square and bisect its lower side. Using the centre point as the centre, and a line from the centre point to each of the opposite corners of the square as the radius, arcs are described to intersect extensions of the lower side of the square. With radii from each of the two intersections to the opposite lower corners of the square obtained in this way and with the lower corners as centres, arcs are described to intersect the extended perpendicular bisector of the lower side of the square. Arcs with centres at the two lower corners of the

The dome of the Mosque of Qaitbay in Cairo displays the sophisticated skills of the masons in the carving of the relief geometric patterns intertwined with arabesques on a surface that is curved in three dimensions. The dome dates from 1472 in the Mamlouk period.

the right-hand number, the result equals the number preceding the pair. Algebraically, the Golden Ratio can be expressed as follows: a:b :: b: a+b. In the twentieth century it has been used by the architect Le Corbusier as the basis of a mathematical system for obtaining two ranges of dimensions (which he called red and blue) suitable for use on any scale in architectural design. He claimed that this system is in sympathetic relation to the dimensions of the human body. The Golden Ratio can be used for determining the dimension of rectangular elements in decorative design and was sometimes used in this way by Islamic designers. It was also used in the setting-out of the ground plans of many historic buildings, both Islamic and pre-Islamic, as were the root 2, root 3 and root 5 ratios.

Critchlow and others explain that the Islamic designers' expert and intricate use of pattern and number is not solely a matter of mathematical manipulation in order to obtain aesthetically pleasing results but also an activity of cosmological significance. This attitude is based on the belief that mathematics has a divine origin and that numbers have a qualitative aspect beyond the quantitative, just as they also have a metaphysical effect. A rotating motif is cited as one of the most common repeat units, the four sides of the square symbolizing the four seasons and the four elements; while the 12 sides of the dodecagon represent the 12 signs of the zodiac. The circle is seen as a timeless whole and the three sides of the triangle symbolize Heaven, Earth and Mankind. Seven is the number of days of the week, whereas six represents the days of Creation. These numbers are cited only as examples; the cosmology of numbers is a highly complex and exhaustive subject and there appears to be little solid evidence that craftsmen consciously used this form of symbolism.

square are then described to intersect the two existing arcs. A pentagon is then obtained by joining the two lower corners of the square to these two intersections and from them to the intersection already obtained with the perpendicular bisector of the lower side of the square.

The sides of a pentagon drawn in this way are equal and the ratio of its diagonal to a side is a very special relationship known as the Golden Ratio. This ratio was known to Euclid and was expressed numerically in the early thirteenth century by the scholar Fibonacci of Pisa by the series 1, 2, 3, 5, 8, 13, 21, 34, 55, 89, 144 and so on, in which, if any pair of consecutive numbers are added together, their value is equal to that of the next number in the sequence. It follows that, if a pair of consecutive numbers is taken from the series and the left-hand number is subtracted from

Opposite: The curved surface of the dome of the Shah Mosque at Isfahan is covered with ceramic tiles in a profusion of arabesques while the drum is encircled with flowing and geometrical calligraphy. The shaft of the minaret is covered with relatively simple geometric patterns. The setting-out of this masterpiece must have required a comprehensive knowledge of geometry. See also illustrations on page 51.

Six examples of Arabic calligraphy.

Top: Flowing calligraphy, both horizontal and circular, on the tiled walls outside the circumcision room at the Topkapi Palace at Istanbul.

Second down: A band of inscription in rectangular Kufic calligraphy over the entrance facade of the Alcázar, the royal palace at Seville which was expanded by Pedro I of Castile. It reads 'There is no victor but Allah'. Note the crosses formed on some of the vertical strokes. These were presumably to please the Christian king who could not read Arabic.

Third down: An elegant incised stucco inscription in Arabic calligraphy from the Court of the Myrtles at the Alhambra, Granada.

Bottom left and right: Glazed ceramic inscriptions in geometric Kufic calligraphy from a tomb at the Shahi Zinda necropolis for Timurid nobles at Samarkand.

Bottom centre: Kufic calligraphy in carved stucco from the Barca gallery which is between the Hall of the Ambassadors and the Court of the Myrtles at the Alhambra, Granada.

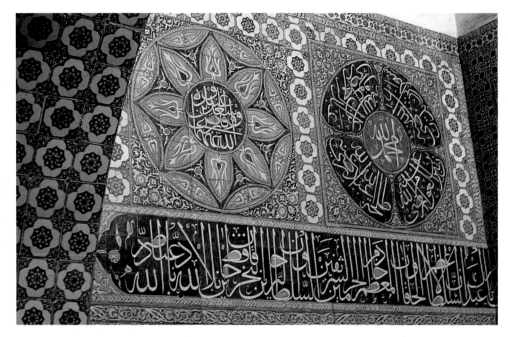

However, within the Islamic world the occurrence of certain geometric patterns does appear to coincide with certain geographic areas. Patterns based on the square and root 2 proportions are common in Spain and Morocco, whereas the pentagon and decagon are frequently found in Isfahan. In the Alhambra a number of patterns based on dodecagons are combined with nine-pointed stars. In Cairo many mimbars have patterns based on the pentagon, and seven-pointed stars are also carved in their timberwork. On many occasions fluid lines were combined with crystalline geometric patterns; examples of curvilinear patterns integrated with hexagonal stars can still be seen in the Alhambra.

Elegant calligraphy is a dominant aspect of the decorative impression created by most Islamic buildings, especially mosques. Those who read Arabic appreciate the religious and poetic value of the inscriptions, and those who do not admire the beauty of the continuous curvilinear pattern they create. Burckhardt has likened the successive lines of an Arabic text to the weft of a cloth, the vertical strokes being the equivalent of the warp and the horizontal strokes the movement of the shuttle forming the weft. The complete effect is of a web of verticals, horizontals, curves and accents.

Arabic is the script of the Holy Koran and, because no illustrations are allowed, its letters have a sacred character for Muslims. Arabic script is phonetic and sounds are represented by means of line, dots and accents. It is read from right to left and from top to bottom. Vowels are not necessarily transcribed, as long as the meaning is clear. The Arabic alphabet consists of eighteen basic letters, rising to a total of twenty-nine characters if the accents and dots sometimes used to indicate vowels are included. In cursive script the letters are joined together. (Arabic is very economic in its use of space compared to the Roman alphabet; Sir Isaac Pitman, an Arabic scholar, used it as the basis for his invention of shorthand writing, reversing it to read from left to right to suit Western convention.) The oldest Arabic script is known as Kufic, after the town of Kufa on the river Euphrates, in Iraq. This type of script is predominantly, and often entirely, angular because it was developed using rectangular bricks and tiles which are the main building materials in the Euphrates Valley. It sometimes incorporates a few slight curves and the main strokes are sometimes interlaced. This script is known as floriate Kufic and is found in books, as well as in inscriptions carved in stucco in many Islamic buildings. The most common type of Arabic script is known as Naskhi and is used for day-to-day handwriting and typesetting. It is a naturally flowing cursive script and its larger version, Thuluth, is used for inscriptions on

Above: An early fourteenth-century glazed tile decorated in lustre from Kashan in Persia. The flowing calligraphic inscription is a phrase from the Koran.

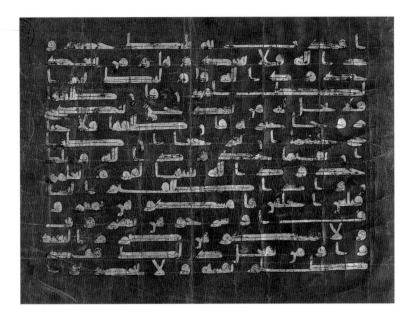

Above left: A Koranic inscription, dating from between the ninth and tenth centuries, written in Kufic with gold ink on vellum.

Above right: A fifteenth-century portrait of a Turkish scribe by Apollonia di Giovanni.

Below: An elegant ceramic sixteenth-century Iznik mosque lamp adorned with flowing cursive script from Ottoman Turkey.

mosques and palaces, often with considerably more elaboration and ornamentation. Two further variations of the script are geographically based: Farsi from Iran and Maghribi from North Africa. Farsi script shows greater variation in the thickness of the line and its flowing horizontal strokes are often slightly curved. Maghribi, on the other hand, has a distinct circular emphasis in its curves, giving an effect of roundness.

One of the most striking decorative uses of Kufic inscriptions is to be found on the drum of the dome and the rectangular bases of the minarets of the Masjid-i-Shah in Isfahan. Here both the curved and flat surfaces are faced with coloured glazed tiles and mosaics. There are also examples in Iran of Kufic calligraphic decoration on walls where the design is based solely on the word 'Allah' repeated in different interlocking settings and delineated in turquoise glaze. The total effect is of almost complete abstraction. A similar effect occurs in a long ornamental frieze running just

below the eaves of the main facade of the Alcázar in Seville. Here the Kufic inscription is delineated in blue and off-white glazed tiles. According to Yousif Mahmoud Ghulam, it reads 'There is no victor but Allah' and was carried out in the fourteenth century by craftsmen from Granada who also added some crosses to please King Pedro, who was not aware of the meaning of the main inscription.

In the Hall of the Ambassadors at the Alcázar, cursive Arabic calligraphy is used extensively as a continuous decorative motif in carved stucco. The use of Kufic for inscriptions is also found on twelfth-century mosques in Iran where the effect depends solely on the use of projecting brickwork. At the Alhambra there is a characteristic link between decoration and calligraphy. In many of the decorative wall panels, where an Arabic sentence appears at the base, the perpendicular strokes of the letters are extended upwards into interlaced patterns above the writing. Sometimes, shorter inscriptions are also incorporated into spaces within the interlaced patterns at a higher level. Inscrip-

A Persian prayer carpet in silk, c.1600, decorated with arabesques and calligraphy. The darker curved line at the centre is a metaphor of the mihrab, indicating the direction of prayer.

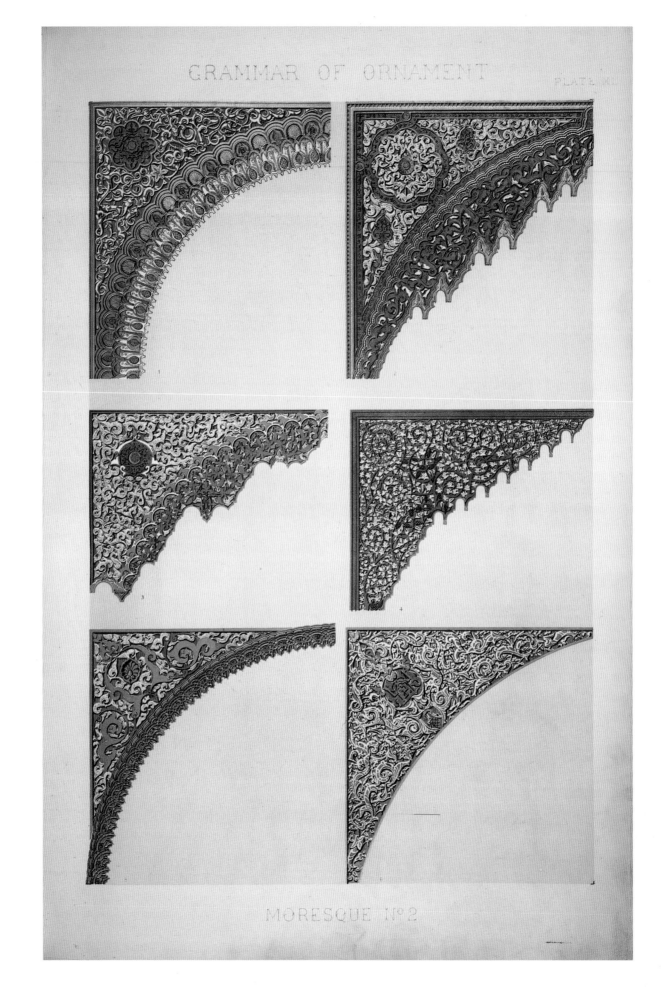

tions of this kind are illustrated in several of the plates in Owen Jones's *Grammar of Ornament*.

Calligraphy in an architectural context is often presented in horizontal friezes of glazed tiles, which are usually blue or turquoise set against a light background. Alternatively, the inscription may be incised in the dark glazed surface of a plain tile, leaving the lighter unglazed body as a background. Most calligraphy, however, is usually carved in relief from stucco, the sunken surfaces sometimes painted in a variety of primary colours.

Apart from its original use in early copies of the Koran and other holy manuscripts, calligraphy was widely used as a decorative device on textiles, metalwork, carved timberwork, ivory, glassware and pottery. In a religious context, besides the surfaces of the religious buildings themselves, it was used to decorate mosque lamps, minbars, carpets and prayer rugs. In a domestic context, Arabic calligraphy of all types frequently decorated dishes, bowls, caskets, ewers, jars and woven textiles. The earliest known architectural inscriptions date from AD 512–13 and are, therefore, pre-Islamic.

It is generally believed that both Arabic and Hebrew developed from the Phoenician alphabet, which was made up exclusively of consonants. Hebrew is the older script, the oldest known examples dating from 1000 BC. (The greater part of the Old Testament was written in Hebrew.) In its early form Hebrew was made up only of consonants and was read from right to left. Although a cursive version has evolved for ordinary daily use, a 'square' version has always been used for official documents, scrolls and calligraphic inscriptions. In the famous synagogue of the Trànsito in Toledo, there is a splendid frieze (1357) carved in stucco with the psalms written in Hebrew calligraphy. It was built and richly decorated in the Mudéjar style, as was the other synagogue to survive in Toledo,

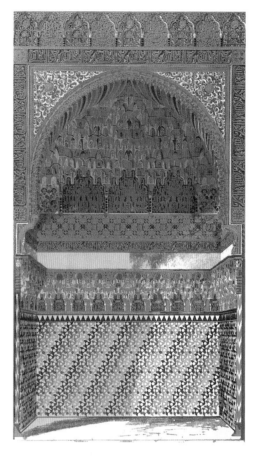

An illustration of an alcove in the Court of the Myrtles at the Alhambra by Owen Jones and Jules Goury. The vivid colours of the carved stucco decoration should be compared with the left-hand photograph on page 95. Jones and Goury believed that they were originally as shown here.

Santa Maria la Blanca. However, when the Moorish style was adopted for synagogues built in the nineteenth century, the rich decorative effect of their interiors was generally achieved without extensive use of calligraphy. A simple inscription over the main entrance usually sufficed.

As for Christian churches built in the Mudéjar style, few interiors have survived in their original form. Artistic representations of divine and human figures were encouraged, and even preferred to calligraphic inscriptions because the majority of the congregation were illiterate. As a result there is little evidence of calligraphy in Roman characters. A magnificent exception is the continuous frieze in

Opposite: Plate 40 in the section of Owen Jones's *Grammar of Ornament* (1856) which deals with 'Moresque Ornament from the Alhambra'. These six examples of the spandrels of arches are taken from various situations in the Hall of the Two Sisters, the Court of the Lions, the Court of the Myrtles and the Hall of Justice.

A sixteenth-century Turkish glazed tile in which the *'cuerda seca'* technique has been used to create a thin dark line between white areas and colours of high intensity and so prevent them merging.

Latin that runs around the cornice below the continuous gallery at the higher level of the throne room of Ferdinand and Isabella of Spain in the palace of the Aljafería at Saragossa.

The remaining element of pattern that plays an essential part in the visual effect created by line, shape, number and the area so decorated is colour as produced by the quality of light reflected from a particular object or surface. Except at sunrise and sunset, sunlight is white and is the sum of all the colours of the spectrum. The possible range of colours is infinite and depends on the source and strength of the light. At sunset the colour of a building, for example, will be perceived as different from its colour at midday, or when it is lit by artificial or natural light. Dark colours absorb more light than do lighter colours.

All natural materials have a colour value but relatively few have colours of high intensity. One exception is the brightly coloured marble used in

the decorative facing of the Taj Mahal at Agra. Usually, if a bright colour is required for aesthetic effect, it is necessary to apply artificial colour in some way. Islamic artists and craftsmen used paint containing strong bright pigments, usually in primary hues. As Owen Jones and others emphasized in their surveys of the Alhambra, the use of polychrome decoration on elaborately carved stucco was a common characteristic of Islamic design. Jones maintained that certain fixed principles were followed here and that they were based on natural laws. First, colour was always used to emphasize form. Secondly, Muslim craftsmen always used primary colours on their stuccowork. The secondary colours were confined to the mosaics and tiles of the dados to provide a point of repose for the eye and some visual relief from the brighter colours at the higher level. Jones admits, however, that at the time of his survey, the background of much of the decoration was green. The reason for

A domed ceiling in a modern religious building in Fez. The colours of the incised stuccowork are very strong and possibly stronger than those used in Moorish buildings such as the Alhambra because only natural dyes were then available.

The use of colour at the Taj Mahal is restrained and subtle because it depends on the contrast between different marbles. There are no applied colours. Above is shown the intricate patterns of the inlaid marbles used on the archway, the frame above and the drum of the dome. Below is a detail of a border decorated with floral arabesques.

this, he asserted, was that the metallic pigments were originally blue and had become green through the passage of time.

Although the decoration at the Alhambra was covered with several thin coats of whitewash, Jones was able to find colour in the interstices by scaling off the whitewash. He discovered that the artists had chosen red, the strongest colour, for the depths of the moulded surfaces where it might be softened by shadow. Blue was used in shaded spots whereas gold was placed on surfaces exposed to light. The colours were separated by

white bands or lines of shadow in order to bring out their true values and to prevent their impinging on each other. Jones was later to employ this same approach to colour in his scheme of decoration for the Crystal Palace at the Great Exhibition in 1851. In his Proposition 28 in *The Grammar of Ornament* he went even further when he stated that colours should never be allowed to impinge on each other, adding other recommendations concerning edgings and outlines. Gold, if used against a coloured ground, should be outlined with black, whereas ornaments of any colour

Opposite: Another detail from the Taj Mahal showing the contrast between white marble carved in relief and a white marble pilaster inlaid with a variety of darker marbles to create geometric linear patterns.

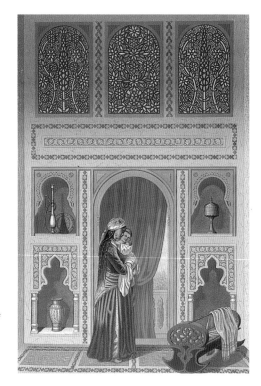

Right: The nursery of the house of Sidi Yusuf Adami in Cairo, as portrayed by Prisse d'Avennes in Volume III of his *L'Art Arabe*. At the top of the arched screen there are three windows with coloured glass set in floral patterns.

Far right: In the Mamlouk house of Gamal El Din Al Dhahabi (1637) in Cairo there is a large *mashrabiyya* window whose upper panels are glazed with coloured sections set in a series of geometric patterns. The contrast in the quality of light is brilliantly depicted in Lewis's painting of a similar house on page 66.

were to be separated from grounds of another colour by edgings of white, gold or black. His Plate 40 shows six details from the spandrels of the arches in the main chambers of the Alhambra in which intricate arabesques are combined with many small-scale *muqarnas* and the colours consist of primary blue and red as well as white and gold. The surfaces of the multi-faceted carved stucco must have sparkled like jewels in the reflected sunlight.

Muslim potters used similar methods in the manufacture of ceramic tiles. In one technique, known as *cuenca* (the Spanish for hollow), the pattern is impressed into the clay, leaving little walls of clay as the outlines so as to prevent different-coloured glazes from intermingling. In another technique, called *cuerda seca* (dry cord), the outlines of the pattern are drawn with a mixture of manganese and grease, which prevents the coloured glazes becoming mixed. Both these methods originated in the Middle East but became characteristic of Hispano-Moorish pottery.

Patterns of all the types already mentioned have been used by skilled weavers from pre-Islamic times to the present day to create beautiful carpets.

These carpets and mats, in which colours ranging from bright primaries to the most subtly subdued tones intermingle, were an essential ingredient in the interior design of the Islamic religious and domestic environment.

The natural colour of stone was used extensively for flooring and for the cladding of walls and domes. Stone was sometimes arranged to form intricate patterns, as in the Taj Mahal, where the stones of curvilinear outline were used, or was used to form geometric repeat units. Strongly coloured marbles were often inlaid against a more neutral stone background to form patterns. The process of inlay was also employed to form geometric patterning in wood panels and caskets by exploiting colour contrasts and differences in grain. Materials such as ebony, bone, ivory and mother-of-pearl were used for the inlaid pattern. The technique survives in the Middle East and North Africa to this day.

A final effect of the use of colour in Moorish style is that produced by light passing through painted or stained glass. The unique luminosity thus produced differs from that of colour reflected from an opaque surface and is due to the translucence of the glass. The perceived pattern, normally geometric, is achieved through the shape and colour contrast of the assembled pieces of glass. These may be held in position by means of a frame made from lead, gypsum plaster or timber. In Morocco, coloured glass windows known as *shemmassiat* are made by embedding pieces of glass in carved gypsum frames. This traditional method is still used today. If coloured glass is used in a window requiring fairly strong light, some areas of transparent glass may be incorporated into the design. This practice was sometimes adopted in the designs of the upper panels of the large balcony windows in the Mamlouk houses of Cairo. When strong sunlight shines directly through a patterned coloured glass window, shafts of sunlight transfer the pattern to interior surfaces which may themselves be decorated with patterns. A magical interaction between them can result; and this will change as the position of the sun changes with the time of day.

Opposite: Two arches in the Court of Lions at the Alhambra decorated in complex relief patterns of latticework and calligraphy in stucco.

Right: A sensitive drawing of a horse in the form of a calligram, dating from 1849 and originating from Iran. The inscription includes the words: 'O King, may the face of the earth be under the hoof of your white horse...and this golden constellation of the firmament the ornament of your saddle. Born to palace service, the aged Sayyid Husayn Ali executed this calligraphy.'

All crafts are customs and colours of civilization. Customs become firmly rooted only through much repetition and long duration.
Ibn Khaldoun

An interior of the Mosque of Sidi Bu Madya at Tlemcen. This watercolour and pencil drawing is a vivid rendering of a religious discussion and shows the minbar and mihrab beyond. It dates from 1881 and the artist is S Fabizi.

Above: This detail of a timber marquetry panel demonstrates the skills of Moroccan woodworkers in the use of inlaid strips of light and dark woods to form interlacing geometric patterns that suggest the third dimension.

Right: The Imam about to turn and deliver the Friday prayer from the minbar at the mosque of Qaitbay in Cairo. This illustration is by Prisse d'Avennes and shows the intricate geometric carving to the woodwork of the minbar.

Although wood is, by its very nature, a perishable material, a vast range of woodwork, carved, turned and assembled in the Islamic tradition, has survived through many centuries to serve as precedents for later generations. The art of making patterns was seen by Islamic craftsmen as a process of forming concepts which were based on a knowledge of the materials. Thus the choice of the appropriate timber was vital. This choice was dependent on availability. In some areas particular woods were rare and, since importing them was expensive, they were treated with special care. Pine and cedar were abundant in Turkey, Syria and Morocco, while plane was grown in Turkey. Hardwoods like teak and ebony were obtained from Sudan, India and Indonesia. Many other species such as walnut, cypress, elm, box, pear, pomegranate, beech and willow were available in Turkey and Persia and were favoured for carving. In the arid regions like the Arabian peninsula there was a very limited supply of timber; only palm and tamarisk.

Muslim woodworkers were respected for their expertise, which was based on a pre-Islamic tradition inherited from Pharaonic Egypt, Persia and Byzantium. Carpenters held a favoured position in the building trades and many became architects, especially in Turkey. This career path is not so surprising, as timber was normally used structurally in Islamic buildings, the decorative elements being added later. While those who undertook inlaid work and made the turned units of the *mashrabiyya* were regarded as specialists, in general no differentiation was made between

carpenters, joiners and cabinet-makers. In the early periods of Islamic art, the decorative patterns were in relief. Bevelling, which gave a more padded or quilted effect, followed later. In the tenth to eleventh century in Egypt, deeper undercutting and beading were introduced.

In mosques used for prayers on Fridays, the minbar, or pulpit, an important feature, is usually made entirely of wood and elaborately decorated with carving. The minbar acts as a metaphor for the function of the Prophet and his Caliphs and is thought by some to be derived from the stepped stool with three levels used by the Prophet in his mosque at Medina. According to tradition the Prophet sat on the third level and rested his feet on the second. Later, after the Prophet's death, the first Caliph sat on the second level and rested

An interior by Prisse d'Avennes of a harem in Tekassir which incorporates a gallery with panels of *mashrabiyya*-type perforated woodwork. Below geometric patterns predominate.

enclosed by handrails, with a canopy at the top level and a doorway at the foot of the stairs. It was placed to one side of the mihrab and was used to demonstrate the design and craft repertoire of the woodworker. The canopy, the doorway, the balustrades and the sides of the staircase were elaborately decorated with relief carving and inlaid work which drew on the full range of geometric and arabesque patterns and calligraphy. The minbar of the Koutoubia mosque in Marrakesh, which was made in Cordoba, Spain, in the twelfth century, is a wonderful example. Its inlaid geometric patterns are both intricate and interlacing and are combined with carved arabesques. Some sixteenth-century Turkish examples incorporated steeply pointed domes over the canopy and these were faced with coloured glazed tiles, often of Iznik design.

In the Islamic house no room was set aside specifically for the serving of food. Squatting on carpets or reclining on cushions piled upon a low platform, male members of the household and their guests took meals and refreshments in the reception space. Female members took their meals in the family area. Chairs were not used until Western influence became predominant from the early nineteenth century onwards among the rich and prominent. Trays and small low tables, usually octagonal and sometimes carved or inlaid with bone, were used in an informal way, as and when required. Only the rich in India had beds in the modern sense; these rested on small wooden feet and were occasionally covered with canopies supported on posts. The Turkish couch, which was stuffed and covered with fine material, was intended for reclining. With the addition of wooden legs, it was adopted in Western Europe in the late seventeenth century and has been a distinct item of furniture ever since. This type of couch, without a

his feet on the first. Other sources, however, maintain that the original minbar had six levels, while the oldest surviving examples have between seven and eleven levels. Custom dictates that the Imam deliver his Friday sermon from one of the lower levels; the upper steps and in particular the topmost one, which is adorned with a headboard, are left empty, symbolizing the pre-eminence of the Prophet. The design of the minbar today follows the continuing tradition of a narrow staircase

back or arms, was referred to as a divan, a word derived from the name of the Turkish council of state, whose members sat on cushions on a low platform, in the traditional Islamic manner. A divan was also sometimes called an Ottoman, especially in France. A more formal version of the divan with a back and two arms was called a sofa and this item has since become an important part of Western furniture design, made in a variety of different styles.

Timber panelling was frequently installed in palaces and domestic settings, as were timber doors and frames. The degree of decoration and carving usually corresponded to the prestige, social position and wealth of the owner. The structure of a building was often made from timber, especially the roof and suspended floors. Timber columns, arches, beams, lintels and ceilings were often decorated but the visual appreciation of their function was never obscured. Perhaps the most sophisticated assembly of wooden elements in domestic architecture was the balcony window known as the *mashrabiyya*, and found in the Mamlouk houses of Cairo. A variety of patterns is created in the latticework by the arrangement of differing shapes and sizes of units. When the sunlight falls on the curved surfaces of the turned wood units, it creates the effect of varying dark and light, thus both reducing glare and resulting in a subtle pattern of line, shape and tone. At the upper level of the window there is frequently a row of panels of coloured glass. The pieces of coloured glass are set in fine gypsum plaster and contained in wooden frames. The patterns are in primary colours, representing arabes-

ques, geometric repeat units, flowers and occasionally peacocks. The overall effect is magical; charmed by it, many European visitors in the nineteenth century brought home dismantled panels which they reconstructed and used as screens or for other decorative purposes in their drawing rooms. Such panels continue to be produced in Egypt and Morocco. The traditional lathe, hand-operated by means of a bow is still in use in Morocco.

Teak imported from Java was the timber used for the *rowshan*, a screen that was a common feature of the large houses of the harbour towns of the Red Sea. It was cut into rectangular slats or laths notched in such a way as to form a latticework fitted into frames. The lattice was based on a grid which was either on the diagonal or on the

Above: A cedarwood lattice window set in a wall of carved stucco decoration at the Bou Inania Madrassa in Fez.

Left: A young turner using his simple lathe to make elements for *mashrabiyya* in Cairo. The bow which turns the wooden unit is operated by his right hand while he holds the blade with his left.

square and was often formed with intricate fretted patterns and carved elements in three dimensions. This lattice-work produced a pattern of light and shade which was different in quality from that of the *mashrabiyya*. The most elaborate type of *rowshan* was crowned with a wide overhanging hood surmounted by a central crest. Simpler types of roof were surmounted by a cornice. As might be expected of such skilled craftsmen, there was a variety of decorated timber elements including doors, internal archways, ceilings and minbars. There were a few examples of painted elements but usually the teak was untreated, although this has not prevented its survival for several centuries. Sadly, Suakin is in ruins today but some traditional houses in a similar style have been preserved in the old quarter of Jeddah in Saudi Arabia.

When used in a repetitive and intricate manner, the *muqarna* was sometimes made from carved timber, usually cedar. It was assembled from a variety of standard units before being fixed to a ceiling or the intrados of an arch. This highly skilled operation required extremely accurate setting-out. Timber *muqarnas* were painted and often gilded. It was common practice to finish the intricate patterns of carved ceilings and wall panels with bright colours and gilding which were carefully integrated into the total design. These skills have survived and can still be found today in Morocco.

In Spain, a Moorish tradition of carpentry skills has been handed down over the centuries. The Mudéjar *artesonado* ceiling with its geometric patterning has affected the vernacular design of panelled doors and ceilings today. The rules that were laid down by municipal authorities to govern the construction of timber roof structures incorporating the decorative ceilings are typified by those writ-

ten in 1619 by Diego Lopez de Arenas, who was the municipal surveyor of Seville and specialized in carpentry. These rules referred to '*la carpintería de lo blanco*' (woodwork) and covered the type of structure, the dimensions of the members to be used, as well as the framework and the decorative patterns of the ceiling. A series of drawings that accompanied the rules showed the layout and the geometric principles involved in the setting-out of the work. This publication appeared after the deportation of the remaining Moors from Spain but by then the Moorish tradition of carpentry had been absorbed into the Spanish architectural tradition and had spread to Spanish colonies in the Americas. Many of the interlacing geometric patterns are directly descended from Islamic precedent.

Stone, the second most important natural material in Moorish architecture, was widely used for structural and decorative purposes. Like timber, it requires only cutting and shaping, but being heavy and thus difficult to handle, it is often cut and shaped at or near the quarry. Normally, only the detailed carving and finishing are done in situ. Because of the difficulty of transporting it, the use of stone as a building material tends to have a regional base. Stone is only carried any great distance if it is rare and particularly needed for its decorative quality. A general characteristic of stone is that it is very strong when compressed but weak when subjected to tensile stress. It is, therefore, rarely used for beams but commonly employed for columns and walling and is cut into wedge-shaped blocks for use in arches, vaults and domes where it is under compression.

The type of stone that is most evident in Moorish buildings is marble. Marble, a crystalline limestone, can take a high polish and a smooth finish and is prized

for the beauty of its colour and grain. It is found in a wide variety of colours ranging from white to dark green and black, the coloured varieties often having especially interesting graining. Throughout the Muslim world, countless examples of marble-work attest to the skills and artistic talents of Islamic masons and sculptors. White marble was used for capitals, grilles and decorative friezes carved with arabesques and calligraphy. Coloured marble was used for inlaid pattern-making, the most notable example being the elegant arabesques and calligraphy of the Taj Mahal at Agra, where dark green and red inlays contrast with the overall background of the ivory-white marble facing.

Sandstone was used structurally and in a decorative manner, though the range of its colours is not as extensive as that of marble. The most intense colour effect is probably that produced by the red sandstone which gives unity to the complex of Mogul buildings at Fatehpur Sikri. In some places, stone that was softer and had a more open grain was used for capitals, *muqarnas* and voussoirs. This gave a textured effect when cut and carved. The stone quarried at Salé, near Rabat in Morocco, is a typical example. Alabaster, a fine-grained form of limestone or gypsum which is easy to carve and translucent if cut into thin sheets, is another type of stone used in Islamic buildings for its decorative potential. Onyx is also occasionally used for its translucent quality. At many coastal sites in the Arabian peninsula, such as on the Red Sea and the Arabian Gulf, coral stone was cut from reefs and shaped into blocks for building load-bearing walls. As it deteriorates if soaked with water, coral stone does not weather well; it was always protected with lime plaster. In the Red Sea towns, walls were also braced with horizontal timber inserts which contributed some tensile strength to combat the effects of settling.

Left: The *artesonado* timber ceiling to the upper storey of the cloister at the monastery of San Juan de los Reyes at Toledo. The monastery was built by Ferdinand and Isabella in celebration of a military victory.

Far left: The carved stucco capital to a column in the Alhambra at Granada with *muqarna* decoration and calligraphy above.

Left: The elaborately carved red sandstone capital of the central column that supports Akbar's throne in the private audience chamber at Fatehpur Sikri. The bracket motifs indicate Hindu influence in this Mogul building.

Opposite: A detail of the floral decoration at the Taj Mahal carved in white marble.

The most common use of gypsum is in the form of a fine plaster known as stucco. This can be moulded or carved into almost any three-dimensional form, either on a brick, random stone or timber backing. Friezes, panels and inscriptions are made in this way. When forming the more complicated shapes, such as those of *muqarnas*, it is sometimes necessary to construct a timber framework to support the laths which hold the plaster in position. In some instances the plaster is moulded on the timber frame, placed in position and then carved in situ, usually before it has completely hardened. After being carved into one of the patterns taken from the extraordinarily extensive repertoire already outlined, it is painted or gilded to give the full decorative effect.

Perforated window grilles (*jalis* or *celosías*) were often made solely from carved gypsum.

When it was desirable to exclude air as well as rain, and to create an attractive pattern of sparkling, translucent colours, shaped pieces of coloured glass filled the voids in the stucco grille. Sometimes, pieces of stone, coloured glass or mother-of-pearl were embedded in the plaster. This was to give emphasis to a particular feature of a pattern which was predominantly stucco. In a mosaic, on the other hand, the function of the plaster is to fix small, usually square, pieces of coloured stone, glass, gold leaf or tile in place and the overall effect of colours and patterns is formed by the pieces themselves. Mosaic techniques were used throughout the centuries by Islamic designers. Their original inspiration came from Byzantine precedent, but they began to use mosaic in a non-figurative manner, particularly in the times of the Umayyad caliphate. This technique was revived

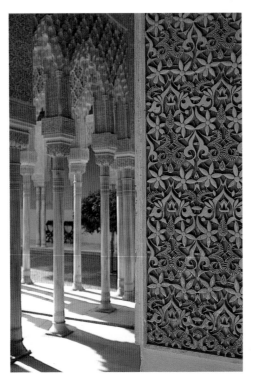

Two details of delicately carved floral and *muqarna* decoration in stucco at the Court of Lions at the Alhambra.

in the late nineteenth century by designers and architects such as Antonio Gaudí. Buildings in Barcelona designed by Gaudí have colourful surfaces, both flat and curved, faced with irregular fragments of glazed tile.

As a building material, clay can be used either in the form of sun-dried bricks or as a damp paste rammed within a wooden framework to form walls which are then allowed to dry and harden. In extremely dry climates and with certain especially chosen types of clay, the eroding effect of the weather has been relatively minor; and some clay buildings in Morocco have survived for many centuries. The external walls of the Alhambra also contain sections of rammed-earth construction. David Hicks has discovered traces of rammed earth behind the stucco decoration of a wall at the western end of the Court of Lions at the Alhambra.

It was soon discovered that if clay bricks were fired in kilns, both their durability and their strength were greatly improved. The burnt brick thus became the preferred material for important buildings in places where stone was not readily available; this was especially true in Mesopotamia and some parts of Morocco and Spain. Islamic builders extended existing Mesopotamian and Roman traditions with their use of burnt clay bricks and tiles for both structural and decorative purposes. Walls, domes, vaults and arches were built in brick, floors were paved and walls faced with burnt clay tiles. The decorative potential of brickwork in relief was developed in Mesopotamia and Persia and elaborate geometric patterns, as well as Kufic calligraphy, were applied in large panels in mosques and palaces. Bricks were cut and special bricks moulded in exceptional shapes and fixed to curved surfaces in *muqarna*-like forms. An example is to be found in the arcade of the Palace in the Qala at Baghdad where shaped bricks are combined with terracotta blocks carved in relief.

These skills found their way westwards to Morocco and Spain. In Aragon, the Mudéjar builders used large-scale panels of brick arranged in geometric patterns to give visual interest to the external walls and bell towers of churches and cathedrals. In some cases the brick patterning incorporated coloured glazed tile inserts, either flat or in the form of roundels, which resulted in a very rich texture giving the impression of a huge tapestry hanging in the urban landscape. The spectacular towers of Teruel, in Spain, are outstanding examples. After the period of the Spanish Inquisition, many Muslim builders fled from Aragon to Tunisia, where they built mosques in brick, employing Mudéjar patterning on the walls of the minarets very similar to that which they had used on the Christian bell towers in Spain.

Another detail of the incredibly complex carved stucco which appears along the top of the glazed ceramic dado in the Court of the Myrtles at the Alhambra.

Another, equally ancient, use of clay is to shape and then fire it to make containers for food and liquids. Thus the craft of pottery is one of the prime indicators of culture. Initially, Islamic pottery for daily practical use was made from clay shaped on the wheel, pressed into a mould or modelled by hand when relief decoration was required. Except in the case of large pots intended for strictly functional use, there was an innate desire for decoration. This could be achieved with designs made by incision with a sharp instrument in the malleable clay and by applying extra pieces of clay to the surface. There was also a stronger urge to apply colour to pottery as a means of decoration. At first, a thin slip of clay coloured with a mineral-based pigment was painted on the vessel before it was fired but it was found that this method was not completely reliable since the slip was sometimes damaged during the firing process. Another problem was that the range of colours that could be created by this process was limited to reds, browns and black.

 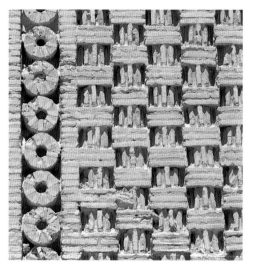

The square domed mausoleum of Ismail Samani at Bukhara. Built in the early tenth century, it is constructed of baked brickwork and uses a variety of geometric patterns. The main facade is shown on the left and a detail of the brick patterning on the right.

Another process was developed to apply colour permanently to the surface of pots, vases, plates and tiles. This was the process known as glazing. A vitreous substance applied to the surface of the object before firing became during firing a thin glassy coating that fused with the surface of the pot. For a clear glaze that did not hide the colour of the body, a mixture of lead, sand and salt was applied. Colours were normally obtained by the addition of metallic oxides. Iron produced yellows and pale pinks, copper made greens and blue-greens, manganese made black and browns, and cobalt produced strong blues. A white glaze was obtained by the use of tin or zinc. Not only could glazing produce an unlimited range of colours but it also rendered earthenware waterproof. This had obvious practical advantages.

Some of the simplest and most refined examples of Islamic earthenware dishes, covered in white slip and decorated with Kufic calligraphy in black or dark brown under a transparent glaze, originate in tenth-century East Persia. In an elegant example in the St Louis Art Museum, the inscription circles the rim of the flat dish, the vertical strokes of the script extending inwards towards the centre. The inscription reads: 'Deliberation before action protects you from regret'. Unlike later Islamic ceramics, the white space contained by the lettering is left plain.

During the twelfth century potters in Persia developed a method of producing a clay which was harder and whiter than earthenware. This is usually referred to as 'frit' and was made by mixing ground quartz with the clay. When fired, the glaze and clay vitrified, or fused together. Because frit is more malleable than clay, and less liable to crumble, the shape into which it could be modelled became more elegant. It was also possible to pot it thinly enough to produce a translucent ware. This ware was often decorated with incised designs under a monochrome glaze. A circular dish from Persia decorated in this way, with a design of birds under a transparent blue glaze, is in the collection of the Victoria and Albert Museum.

Another type of glaze developed at this time was lustre. A compound of sulphur, silver and copper oxides was painted on the fired tin glaze and then fired again in the kiln, giving a thin metal-

Above: A facade of the Mudéjar tower of San Martin at Teruel showing the colourful range of patterns in brick and coloured ceramics.

Right: A close-up of the bell openings of the tower of the church of San Salvador at Teruel, a town which is still renowned for its ceramic production. The interlacing brick patterns over the arches below are also remarkable.

Overleaf: A close-up of the simple coloured glazed brick patterning on the shaft of an unfinished minaret at Khiva in Uzbekistan. Although probably built in the eighteenth century, its style derives from fourteenth-century precedent.

lic lustrous film, reminiscent of gold. It has been suggested that the technique of lustre may have been borrowed from the glassmakers of Syria and Egypt, who had used it as early as the end of the eighth century. Lustre wall tiles were produced at Kashan and Rayy, in Persia. Many were formed in the shape of an eight-pointed star or other interlocking shapes with inscriptions running around the border of each tile. The design sometimes included human and animal figures. Lustreware was also made in Spain. El Idrisi, in an account of his travels during 1150 called *The Book of Roger*, mentions the export of lustreware from Calatayud, in Aragon. During the next century, Malaga became famous for its 'golden wares' and the many lustre wall tiles in the Alhambra were probably made there. Ceramics of all kinds were produced in Moorish Spain. Lustreware continued to be made by Mudéjar potters at several centres in Spain after the Reconquest.

Inspired by costly white porcelain imported from China, the Abbasid court at Baghdad encouraged the development of new wares. Not only was *petunse* (a porcelain clay) not available locally; the technique of making porcelain was a secret closely guarded by the Chinese. As a substitute a glaze that would create a white opaque finish was developed and applied to pottery. The addition of tin to the former lead glaze resulted in a white background on which designs could be painted that remained firm and clear after firing. Simple designs and inscriptions in blue and green against white became very popular on all kinds of vessels, plates and flat tiles for floors and walls.

During the sixteenth century, one of the most celebrated centres of ceramics was Iznik, in Turkey, where a highly sophisticated range of pottery and tilework was created for court, domestic and architectural uses. The beauty of Iznik pottery is unsurpassed. The unifying characteristic of the ware

Two panels of Persian lustre-glazed tiles in low relief, dating from early fourteenth-century Kashan. The tile on the left is figurative, representing King Bahram Gur hunting while his favourite Azada plays the harp. The panel on the right has a geometric basis and incorporates octagonal star tiles with bird, floral and calligraphic elements.

is an underglaze decoration of flowing natural patterns on a pure white ground. The style developed through three successive phases. During the first phase, cobalt blue was the predominant colour, decoration taking the form of floral scrolls in the Islamic tradition, with rims and borders decorated in the Chinese manner. Pottery of the second phase, once thought to be Syrian in origin and therefore called 'Damascus', exhibits an extension of the palette to include greens, pale purple and black as well as a wider range of flowers, now comprising the tulip, hyacinth, carnation, pomegranate and some fanciful, composite forms. Exquisite tiled panels from this phase are to be seen in the Topkapi Sarai in Istanbul. The third phase is usually known as 'Rhodian' because it was once thought to have been made on the island of Rhodes. The palette was extended further to include a variety of reds, but purple disappears. Floral motifs tend to be more realistic than in the Damascus wares. Innumerable examples of Iznik bowls, dishes, plates, cups, jars, jugs and vases exist in museum collections worldwide. Some of the best examples of Rhodian Iznik pottery are the tile panels with Koranic inscriptions in the Suleimaniye Mosque in Istanbul.

Intricate geometric and curvilinear patterns can be created by cutting coloured glazed tiles into an infinite variety of shapes and then arranging them to form a predetermined design. The edges are polished and the pieces (called *zillij* in Arabic) are assembled, glazed side down, according to a drawn

Above: Another panel of lustre-glazed tiles, also from Kashan but dating from the previous century. These tiles are not in relief but have arabesque patterns within an octagonal star framework.

Below: A Persian octagonal star lustre tile of the thirteenth century with a picturesque female figure.

Two examples of Turkish Iznik pottery. Above is a vase of the first phase, which dates from the late fifteenth century, while below right is shown a bowl of the second, so-called Damascus phase. Both are decorated with arabesque motifs.

pattern. A mixture of lime and cement is then poured over them and left to set. The resulting rectangular panels are then applied to wall surfaces by means of another layer of plaster. Columns and other curved surfaces are usually covered by applying the *zillij* directly onto wet plaster. Floors are often paved with glazed rectangular bricks (known as *bejmat*) whose dimensions are 15 cm x 5 cm. They are set in a mixture of lime and cement, laid in square, zigzag or crisscross patterns and occasionally in combination with more complicated patterns made up of cut *zillij*. Fez is the chief centre of these skills in Morocco. In Tetuan, further north, possibly because of the influence of Andalusian immigrants and later Spanish colonial policy, a different technique is used. Tiles are cut or shaped before they are glazed. The *cuerda seca* and *cuenca* methods, as described in Chapter Four, were also adopted, especially in the 1930s, when the Spanish administration set up a crafts school there. The *cuerda seca* method of creating patterns is quicker than *zillij* but the separating lines are thicker and so those who favour *zillij* maintain that *cuerda seca* is less refined and less subtle. This skill has been demonstrated in numerous mosques and palaces from Spain to Persia and India and it reached a particularly high standard in Spain and Morocco in the fourteenth and fifteenth centuries. It still survives today in Morocco, where glazed tiles 10 cm square are cut into geometric or curved shapes by hand on site.

As for wall and floor tiles, these survive in situ in countless palaces and religious buildings throughout the Islamic world, many still serving their original purpose and others being carefully conserved for the pleasure of visitors. Some out-standing tilework has been taken out of Islamic buildings. Conversely, other examples have been removed, and therefore saved, from buildings that no longer exist.

Precious stones and the mystique surrounding them were part of the heritage of the ancient Classical world. The technique of carving and engraving them was known and practised from pre-Islamic times and continued to be developed by Islamic craftsmen, although precise details of their working methods are not recorded. Rock crystal and gems were chipped, sawn and carved to produce objects of use and display. Because there is no priesthood in Islam, there was no ecclesiastical patronage of the arts, and it was princes and wealthy merchants who commissioned craftsmen to create the highly decorated objects of which the finest Islamic lapidary art largely consists. Most early examples are fashioned from crystal, a very hard form of quartz which, when polished, possesses a transparency and sparkle superior to glass. Fatimid Egypt had a reputation for the carving of crystal which, it is believed, was imported from East Africa.

A crystal lamp in the shape of a boat, dating from the Fatimid period and now in the Hermitage Museum, St Petersburg, is decorated with a floral scroll and a border of pearl-like shapes. When lit, it must have shone with a sparkling beauty. The action of light as it passes through crystal also made it an attractive container for transparent liquids, and many crystal goblets, small flasks, jars and bottles were decorated with all forms of incised patterns. Chessmen carved from crystal were a popular product of the craftsmen of Fatimid Egypt, and

A panel of multi-coloured tiles from the seventeenth-century royal palace, known as Chehel Situn or the Hall of Forty Columns, at Isfahan. The '*cuerda seca*' technique was used in the manufacture of these tiles.

many were exported to European countries. The industry was relatively short-lived, however, and was not to re-emerge until the seventeenth century in India under Mogul patronage.

Jade, believed by the Turks to have magical qualities, was probably introduced to the Islamic world from China via Persia. Jade-carving became an important craft in Persia in the fifteenth century and passed to India in the seventeenth, again because of Mogul patronage. Ornamental bowls and cups shaped from jade and decorated with inlaid gold and precious stones were created for the wealthy citizens of Ottoman Turkey and Mogul India.

Glass, which unlike rock crystal is a man-made substance, can easily be shaped and manipulated in its semi-molten state. It is made by fusing a silica-like sand or flint with an alkali such as soda or potash. Before the Romans discovered how to make colourless glass, all glass was coloured in some way. The glass industry was well established in pre-Islamic times and the methods of producing the full range of colours were known. Although glass-making, including the technique of glass-blowing, was flourishing in Syria during the Umayyad period, it was not until the Abbasid dynasty developed its capital at Baghdad that the demand for artistic wares began to grow and a distinctive style began to appear. Cut decoration on colourless glass was developed, sometimes in imitation of carved rock crystal. Colourless glass was also sometimes overlaid with green or blue. Painting with lustre was first evident in Egypt. Gilding and enamelling became a characteristic of Syrian and Egyptian glass of the twelfth and thirteenth centuries and these techniques were employed to decorate the lamps that hung from the ceilings of holy places, many of which were made to the order of a sultan or high dignitary for presentation

to a particular mosque. These exquisite mosque lamps were decorated with a combination of abstract patterns, arabesques and the dominant Koranic inscriptions in elegant cursive Arabic calligraphy. One example of such an inscription is the Koranic verse from the *Sura of Light*, which reads:

Allah is the light of the heavens and the earth; his light is like a niche in which is a lamp in glass and the glass like a brilliant star, lit from a blessed tree…

A parrot forms the main motif for a panel of Iznik tiles from the second or Damascus stage of the sixteenth century.

Opposite: A panel of Iznik tiles (dated 1575) from the third or 'Rhodian' phase from the baths at the mosque of Eyub Ensari on the Golden Horn at Istanbul. Eyub Ensari was reputed to have been the standard-bearer of the Prophet Mohammed and to have died during the Arab siege of Constantinople in 674–8.

This combination of decorative motifs was adopted for a range of containers for domestic use including bowls, beakers, flasks and sprinklers. With the return of the Crusaders, some of these reached Europe where they became highly prized objects.

Although glass has been used in windows since the earliest period of Islam, few glazed windows have survived. Some buildings in Cairo, dating from the thirteenth century, have windows with coloured glass inserts, as, for instance, do the high-set windows in the *madrassa* of Sultan Qala'un. In Iran, the sumptuous interior of the music room within the palace pavilion of Ali Qapu at Isfahan has both stained-glass windows and gilded stucco dating from the early seventeenth century. The domed mosques of the Ottomans had many glazed windows which contained a mixture of both clear and coloured glass. Abstract patterns in colour with a geometric base were usually set in the window so that the clear glass predominated at the highest levels. This arrangement did not produce such a rich effect as the figurative stained-glass windows of the medieval Christian cathedrals but it did allow a higher level of natural light to illuminate the elaborate patterns and calligraphy on the curved faces of the dome and the walls, as well as on the vast horizontal surface of luxuriant colours of the carpets and prayer mats. On a lesser scale, coloured glass panels were used at the upper level in the *mashrabiyya* windows of the larger houses of Mamlouk Cairo but with a higher proportion of coloured glass. The glass was set in lead and fixed to the timber in panels. At earlier periods the glass was often set in plaster grilles in a fashion similar to the small pieces of glass set in opaque mosaic panels, but allowing the light to pass through the glass.

In metalworking, as in other fields of culture, the Arabs inherited a sophisticated tradition from

This late tenth-century ewer is made from rock crystal and originates from Fatimid Egypt. The elegant patterning incorporates a bird of prey and an ibex.

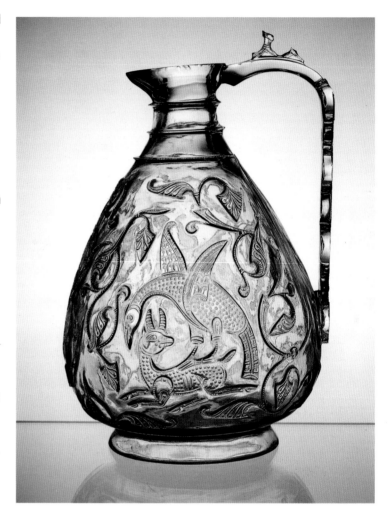

Byzantium and Persia. Harder metals like iron, steel, bronze and brass, used in a structural capacity, were often combined with softer metals such as gold, silver or copper, used decoratively. Part of this tradition are liturgical vessels, articles of personal adornment and a royal crown made from gold set with precious stones which survives from the Visigothic kingdom of Toledo. The first decorative innovation after the foundation of Islam was the addition of Kufic inscriptions to dishes, trays, jugs and bowls. Fine arms and armour, valued highly in Muslim countries since the early period of Islam, were normally decorated. Both daggers and swords were personalized with inscriptions and arabesques, etched on the metal or sometimes inlaid in gold. Damascus was a centre famed for its production of decorated arms and metalwork of all kinds, and the process of giving a watered pattern to steel, in particular sword blades, was known as 'damascening'. Very hard carbon steel was heated and maintained at a high temperature for a long time, allowed to cool slowly and then reheated in a current of air, with intermittent forging. After the final forging, the blade was immersed in acid. The acid etched the steel to reveal a greyish watered effect which contrasted with the polished surface of the steel.

In addition to a wide variety of functional objects for domestic use such as dishes and trays, many animal figures were cast in bronze. Although primarily decorative, some of the cast animal figures were hollow and used to contain water for ablution purposes. These vessels were known as *aquamaniles*. Perhaps the most remarkable example is an *aquamanile* from Persia, in cast bronze inlaid with silver. It is in the form of a zebu cow suckling her calf with a lion attacking her from behind. An inscription on the cow's neck and head reads:

> This cow, calf and lion were all three cast at one time with the help of God, the just, the nourisher, by the labour of Ruzba Ibn Afridun Ibn Barzin to its owner, Shah Barzin Ibn Afridun Ibn Barzin.

with the date 1206 and the name of the decorator. Larger bronze figures were made to serve as fountain heads, with jets of water emerging from the mouths of lions, deer and other animals.

Examples from Fatimid Egypt and Moorish Spain have survived and fountain heads mounted on a basin with statues of gold inlaid with pearls are thought to have existed at a palace of the Umayyad caliphate in Medinat Al Zahra. The lion figures on the most celebrated surviving Andalusian fountain, that of the Court of Lions at the Alhambra, are carved from stone, however.

Cast bronze and brass were also used to make door knockers, lamp stands and candlesticks but the most common metal for domestic articles was brass. Trays and table tops and containers of every kind were made from beaten brass, sometimes used in the form of thin sheets. More elaborate articles bore long and often wordy inscriptions which could take the form of flattering compliments or lists of attributes desirable for the future well-being of the owner. One such list from a beaten brass tray made in thirteenth-century Persia reads:

> Glory, prosperity, wealth, happiness, [God's] support, entirety, [Muhammed's] intercession, perpetuity, sufficiency, honour, tranquillity, gratitude, mastery, victory, superiority, mercy, ease, health, favour, potency, power, sympathy, safety, charity, long life and perpetual commendation to its owner.

In a society where social gatherings and meals took place at floor level, such trays ful-

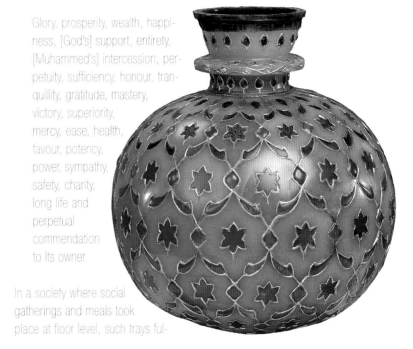

Below: A Mogul huqqa flask made from jade and inlaid with precious stones in gold settings. Its date is not certain but is probably late sixteenth to early seventeenth century.

An illustration from a 1300 Syrian manuscript of the Fatimid period showing Abu Zayd preaching in the mosque at Samarkand. Abu Zayd was a trickster who was portrayed in *The Assemblies* by Al Hariri. Mosque lamps suspended on chains are clearly shown hanging from the arches.

filled an important function and were sometimes placed on low folding carved wooden supports. In a society too where the written word was valued more highly than the image, it is not surprising that the pen box was often regarded as a very special possession. Many pen boxes were made from inlaid wood but the most ornate were formed from beaten brass or bronze and usually had compartments for pens, writing materials and an inkpot. Almost every surface where it was practical to do so was decorated in some way, usually with callig-

raphy and arabesques, although in some examples from Iran formalized human figures form part of the composition.

Textiles were an integral element in Moorish interiors. Islamic peoples had access to an abundance of silk, wool and dyestuffs, the essential raw materials of weaving, and a long history of excellence in textile design has existed among them. Since medieval times so-called Oriental carpets have been exported throughout the world and many of the patterned silk textiles used in medieval

Europe were woven by European craftsmen. In the finest textiles, the pattern is not added to the cloth with the needle after weaving but is woven into the textile as it is made. The finest Oriental carpets, knotted pile carpets, are made by this method. Warp threads are stretched vertically on the loom and the weft threads interlaced horizontally. The pile is constructed by knotting short individual strands around the warp threads. After each row is knotted, a weft thread is carried across the full width of the web and beaten firmly into place with a heavy comb. The strands of each knot, later sheared to create an even pile, appear as a spot of colour in the total surface of the carpet. In this way, the pattern is constructed just as a mosaic is made up from an arrangement of cubes. This system is well suited to weaving with wool or silk. For fine silk textiles required for dress or domestic furnishings, another method is frequently used. As the weaver interlaces the coloured weft threads with the warp threads across the full width of the drawloom, an assistant operates a system of cords that ensures that a coloured thread only appears on the front of the fabric when it contributes to the required pattern. This system is especially suited to the weaving of repeat units across the width and length of the fabric.

Weaving was, and remains to this day, a highly organized industry. Large carpets were woven by several weavers working alongside each other, following a pattern made by a specialist designer who might also have been a painter. Two traditions, the Persian and the Coptic, were absorbed into the work of Islamic weavers. Two religious themes occur in Islamic textile design; one is the garden of Paradise, which is found in carpet designs of the early period, and the other is the arch motif, which is found in some form or other in the design of all prayer rugs. The arch symbolizes the mihrab

A glass mosque lamp dating from 1309 and originating from Syria. The beautiful enamelled inscription includes the dedication to the Mamlouk Sultan Baybars II, together with quotations from the Koran.

and is used to indicate the direction of Mecca.

Carpets were first introduced into mosques at Damascus during the Umayyad dynasty. It was obligatory for the faithful to remove their shoes before entering the prayer area, where each man knelt or sat directly on the carpet. The carpets were never intended to be hung vertically as wall decoration but were meant to be used as floor coverings, forming a horizontal surface in relatively large spaces where they would be viewed from a standing or sitting position. There was a conse-

Opposite: Details of the decoration and calligraphy of the pen box of the Bahri Mamlouk Sultan Shaban as rendered by Prisse d'Avennes. It was made of brass inlaid with gold and silver.

Below right: A Turkish steel helmet of 1500 decorated with damascened silver and designed to fit over a turban.

quent bias towards two-dimensional design with the use of repetitive patterns that were infinitely extensible. Carpets, rugs and cushion covers were also adopted for use in courtly and domestic quarters, and their design became a source of both pleasure and prestige. Whereas in the mosque textile floor coverings were intended to create a rich background to worship and the saying of prayers, in the palace or the home they were used to complement the fine silk textiles that made up the elaborate costumes of court nobles or, at the other end of the social scale, the modest white cotton robes of the ordinary citizen.

The Arabs brought silk production to Spain, and Almería, Málaga, Seville and Granada became centres of silk-weaving. Some interesting fragments of silk textile have survived at the cathedral of Roda de Isabeña, near the northern frontier of Spain. One, dating from the tenth or eleventh century and believed to be of Persian origin, is part of a shroud. It is decorated with a repetitive pattern of medallions with a border incorporating Kufic calligraphy. The colours are red, yellow, white and brown, with red and yellow predominating. Perhaps the most interesting survival is the twelfth-century mitre of Bishop San Ramon, which has borders of woven silk strips of Spanish Islamic workmanship. The irony of using Muslim fabrics for Christian burial and liturgical purposes has never been fully explained but can probably be accounted for by the trade that took place across the religious divide and the travels of clerics with the Christian armies in their forays into Muslim territory. So superior was the quality of Islamic weaving to anything produced in northern Europe at that period that Muslim fabrics were often presented as gifts to prominent nobles and churchmen. The richness and variety of the dyes that were used in these fabrics is illustrated in another exam-

ple from Roda de Isabeña. This fragment dates from the thirteenth century and is of Spanish Islamic origin. It displays a repetitive rhomboid pattern on a brilliant blue background with a contrasting design of red diamonds and yellow flowers. It is believed that this textile also had borders with Kufic inscriptions originally.

Birds and animals were common motifs in Spanish and Turkish textile design from the eleventh to the thirteenth century but were later replaced by geometric and plant patterns in Spain, where there was an increasing production of knotted-pile carpets. In Turkey, a characteristic form of knotting, known as the Turkish, or Ghiordes knot, developed. This is different from the method that was used in Persia and which is usually referred to as the Persian knot. Turkish carpets of the eleventh to thirteenth century frequently had geometric borders, sometimes in a form of pseudo-Kufic. During the fifteenth century in Egypt, outstandingly beautiful carpets were produced using the Persian knot, although Egypt was by then under Turkish domination. These carpets had complex centralized patterns of stars and polygons in red, green and light blue. By the sixteenth century, the golden age of the Ottoman dynasty, the Turkish textile industry was exporting carpets and fine textiles to a world market. An illustration of this is Hans Holbein's famous multiple portrait *The Ambassadors* (now in the National Gallery, London), which features a Turkish carpet with a floral border and a large central octagon. At this time the tulip

became a common motif in Turkish textile design, being particularly popular for kaftans and tomb covers. Dress indicated rank in the Ottoman social system. Turbans of varying degrees of elaboration were of many different colours and patterns, while kaftans were decorated with luxuriant designs similar to those used for Iznik pottery. The urge for display extended to the military. Campaign tents were decorated with intricate coloured appliqué patterns.

Meanwhile in Persia, the trend was for more pictorial subjects, including hunting scenes, which reflected increasing skills in the painting of minia-tures. Kashan and Isfahan became centres for the production of textiles brocaded with metal threads and knotted pile carpets woven in silk. Persian textiles reached a zenith of excellence during the sixteenth and seventeenth centuries, and many luxurious articles of clothing in silk and velvet were exported to Europe.

As might be expected, Persian naturalism spread eastwards to India with the Mogul invasion. The design of the Mogul carpet often took the form of a painting with floral patterns incorporated in the design, for, as in Persia, there was a parallel with miniature painting. In Bengal, cotton was finely woven and in Kashmir to the north, woollen shawls were woven from goat hair. The shawl was adopted at the Mogul court and, often featuring the curvilinear pattern that was later to be known as the paisley pattern, was exported to Europe. Shah Jehan favoured carpets with floral patterns; Aurengzeb preferred lattice designs with subordinate plant motifs. The textile industries of India, Iran and Turkey are still flourishing and they continue to export carpets on an international scale. Although traditional designs survive, manufacture often depends on modern methods and man-made materials such as synthetic dyes. Consequently, the quality of the past is not always maintained. In any case, traditional dress for males, except for religious usage, has been largely superseded by Western-style clothing.

This miniature is believed to be the work of Sayyid Ali, an apprentice of Bihzad, and to have been executed for Shah Tahmasp. It illustrates a scene from the *Khamsa*, in which the skeletal Majnoun is brought from the desert to the tent of Laila. The tents are decorated with multi-coloured patterned fabrics.

This large Persian carpet in wool pile from the second half of the seventeenth century presents a detailed picture map of a luxurious formal garden with flowering trees.

A Mogul miniature of 1658 showing the emperor Aurengzeb at prayer on a floral patterned carpet. He was renowned for being pious and puritanical, in reaction to the immoderate luxury of his father Shah Jehan.

From the earliest period of Islam, calligraphy was considered to be the dominant art. Thus Arabic script and the books which contained it enjoyed a unique status, being held in higher esteem than painting and the decorative arts. The most accomplished calligraphers of the later Islamic period were the Ottomans. They developed a form of monogram, known as the *tugra*, for official royal usage on documents, proclamations, coins and inscriptions on prominent buildings. It usually incorporated the name of the sultan and of his father, the word 'Khan' and a complimentary phrase such as 'ever victorious'. These monograms were elegantly designed and more elaborate than their Western equivalents. European influence, however, began to be evident in miniature painting as an increasing degree of naturalism was introduced.

Pictorial art was debarred from Islamic religious buildings, though stylized plant motifs, the nearest approximation to figurative art, were tolerated. Palaces, on the other hand, often contained figurative paintings, although these were not usually displayed on the walls. There is no specific passage in the Koran that forbids pictorial art but the Hadith or written traditions are hostile to the representation of living forms. In his assessment of the mural paintings in the Qusair Amra, a hunting lodge built in Jordan by a prince of the Umayyad dynasty who later became Walid II in 743, Creswell was of the opinion that the prohibition of painting did not exist in the earliest period of Islam but was gradually established from the end of the eighth century. He suggested that the influence of the Jews who were converted to Islam and the presence of the Iconoclasts at the court of the Umayyads, as well as the feeling that the maker of an image acquires magical powers over the person depicted, may have contributed to the change in attitude. The murals at Qusair Amra, which have

recently been renovated, include renderings of the constellations on the domed ceilings of the bath house, as well as scenes of hunting and dancing in other parts of the building. The most interesting, from an historical point of view, is a mural depicting the so-called Kings of the Earth or the Enemies of Islam. They have been identified as the kings

of Byzantium, Persia and Abyssinia, and Roderic,
the Visigothic king of Spain.

In later periods, pictures in miniature versions
were kept in books or albums. A charming example illustrates the story of Bayad and Riyad and
their torments of love; in the garden Riyad plays
the *oud* (the forerunner of the medieval lute) and
in the background a *mashrabiyya* is clearly depicted. This is considered to suggest a Spanish background and the miniature is thought to date from
the thirteenth century. In Persia the classic period
of the book was the fifteenth century and Herat
was its main centre. This was an age which had
parallels with Renaissance Italy in that patronage of
the arts was associated with political instability and
violence. A wide variety of subjects, with single figures and groups usually in an architectural setting,
was often derived from narrative poems. A colourful example in the National Library in Cairo demonstrates the complete range of patterns of Islamic
interior design. It is based on an episode from
the poem by Jami on the theme of Yusuf and

Zulaykha and is signed by the
artist, Bihzad, the most prominent painter of the Herat
school. Yusuf is shown fleeing
from the attentions of Zulaykha
through seven doors which she
had previously locked but which
had miraculously opened in
response to Yusuf's prayer. Historical themes also featured as
the story line of court albums,
particularly during the Safavid
era. Such a theme illustrating
military and political events was
called a Shahnameh. Safavid
miniatures reflected the great
confidence of the regime and
were executed with a high level of finish and
detail. Single pictures were often commissioned by
courtly patrons, while miniatures were occasionally
copied and enlarged to be hung on palace walls.
There are a few in the Ali Qapu at Isfahan and one
survives in a better state in Chehel Sutun.

Miniature paintings were a form of art enjoyed
by courtiers and the privileged. They were painted
in gouache incorporating a wide variety of natural pigments mixed with gum arabic which was
applied to prepared paper, cloth or vellum.
Because the paintings were brought out only for
inspection on social occasions, their size was limited to one that was convenient for holding in the

that period. By the time of Suleiman there were over forty court painters, and their themes included hunting and military campaigns. Detailed picture maps of Istanbul were also produced. In most of these paintings the Persian landscape style formed the structure of the composition, while the European techniques of realistic shading were absorbed to produce a characteristic Ottoman miniature.

Persian influence on miniature painting in India narrowly preceded the Moguls during the period of the Delhi Sultanates. It was further extended when Persian painters came to India to give the Mogul emperor Akbar personal tuition in the art. This was the beginning of the celebrated Mogul school. A major undertaking of Akbar's workshop in Fatehpur Sikri was the preparation of 1,400 separate illustrations of the Hamzanameh, stories of the uncle of the Prophet Mohammed. Each one was painted on cotton stiffened with card. Akbar was tolerant of Hindu culture and religion and commissioned the translation of the *Mahabharata* and other Hindu epics into Persian, the language of the court. These were illustrated with miniatures prepared in the workshop, at which a staff of 100 eventually worked.

In 1580 the Jesuits brought religious paintings in the European Mannerist style to the Mogul court. A form of symbolism and an emphasis on the individual then became discernible in the work of the court painters. Jahangir was similarly fascinated by aesthetics and also became interested in natural history. The English ambassador, Sir Thomas Roe, brought with

Below: This realistic portrait of the Ottoman Sultan Mehmet was painted by Gentile Bellini in 1480 when he was invited to visit the Ottoman court in Istanbul.

hand. Only in exceptional circumstances did such painting take an enlarged form as murals to decorate palace interiors. A notable example is to be found in the Hall of Justice off the Court of the Lions at the Alhambra. Here, there is a series of portraits of the Sultans of Granada painted on leather and fixed to the ceiling. It is believed that they date from the reign of Yusuf and may have been painted by Christian artists.

In 1480 Gentile Bellini was invited by Sultan Mehmet to visit his court and paint his portrait. The result is realistic in style and shows a confident sultan in considerable facial detail. Bellini was one of the many Italian painters who visited Turkey at

him examples of miniature painting from his country and Jahangir instructed his court painters to copy the English style. It was said that Sir Thomas could not distinguish between a Mogul copy and an English original when they were shown to him. He was presented with an autographed portrait of Jahangir which he was to give to King James I on his return to London. By the reign of Shah Jehan, painting had become more formal and less colourful, possibly because the Sultan was more interested in architecture and in jewellery. This change is evident in the illustrations to the *Padshahnameh*, an account of the exploits of Shah Jehan. They are attributed to an artist called Mancher. When

Shah Jehan was deposed by Aurengzeb in 1658, the arts entered a period of neglect due to his lack of interest and strict religious puritanism. Many artists fled to provincial courts.

In this way miniature painting survived but became increasingly Europeanized especially from the mid-eighteenth century onwards, when the British, through the power of the East India Company, effectively ruled India. What was known as the 'Company Style' was very popular with the new colonials. Figurative painting has persisted from the earliest period of Islam to the present day, although at times it has been actively discouraged by the religious authorities.

A painting in the 'Company Style' of the gateway to Akbar's mausoleum at Sikandra near Agra. The artist has endeavoured to adopt a realistic European manner but has not managed to reproduce the grace and proportions of the subject and the chamfered corners have eluded him. The tops of the minarets, which have now been restored, seem to have been missing when he made his sketches.

This miniature of 1590 captures the splendour of the Mogul court when Akbar was holding a durbar in honour of a nobleman. It is an illustration to the manuscript of the *Akbarnama*, the official history of Akbar's reign, and represents the acme of the Akbar school of miniature painting.

Opposite: A close-up of the pointed domes and pinnacles of the Royal Pavilion at Brighton. John Nash's fantastic arrangement of architectural elements is more fanciful than most of the Mogul originals.

Right: A formalized peacock motif from a page of 'Moorish' designs from *Suggestions in Design* (1880) by John Leighton.

In splendour did the Orient
Cross the Mediterranean Sea;
You must know and love Hafiz
If you are to know the songs of Calderón.
Goethe

A portrait of James Silk Buckingham and his wife, dressed in a version of Moorish costume. Buckingham was a diplomat and adventurer who lived from 1786 to 1855. He collected books and drawings from Persia and was the founder of the *Athenaeum* journal.

The foundation of the East India Company on the last day of 1600 marked the beginning of a relationship between Britain and the Indian sub-continent that has lasted to the present day. Initially a matter of trade and later, colonialism, the relationship soon developed a cultural dimension that was to lead to mutual influences in the decorative arts, design and architecture. Travellers and merchants who returned from India brought vivid descriptions of the magnificent Mogul palaces, mosques and tombs, and they related tales of a colourful and luxurious life at court. James I, who was particularly impressed with the quality of Eastern silks, appointed Sir Thomas Roe as his ambassador at the court of Jahangir, the Great Mogul. Roe spent four years in India following the emperor on his travels through his dominions. On his return he brought back a portrait of Jahangir, as well as descriptions of his experience of India.

However, the taste for the exotic was not entirely new; it had already been established by the merchants of the Levant Company, which had been founded in 1581 with a charter granted by Queen Elizabeth I. An expanding trade in textiles was followed by the import of coffee beans from Aleppo and Mokha in the Yemen. During the seventeenth century coffee-drinking became popular in London, especially among intellectuals, and many coffee houses were opened. Towards the end of the century a number of Turkish baths were built. Whereas the interior of a coffee house was not considered to require any form of exotic decoration, a Turkish bath, on the other hand, had specific needs, notably privacy and surfaces resistant to steam and hot running water. Following in the Oriental tradition, the use of coloured glazed tiles on walls and floors was both functional and decorative, providing a sense of occasion as well as the opportunity to introduce a 'Turkish Mode' in the design of these baths.

As early as 1611, the Reverend John Cartwright in his *Preacher's Travels* had given a description of the rich materials used in the decoration of the royal palace at Isfahan, which had only recently been completed. The complexity of the design of carpets imported from Persia and Turkey, often through Venice, was familiar to the European upper classes, who enjoyed their flowing linear patterns and vigorous use of colour. Indeed, a book of so-called 'Moresque' designs had been published in London by Thomas Geminas as early as 1548. The European taste for Persian and Turkish rugs and carpets, widespread during the seventeenth century, can also be observed in portraits by Holbein, Van Dyck and Rubens. Considerable influence came by way of Holland, where the fashion for Oriental dress was strong. Glazed tiles made at Delft and decorated with tulip patterns in underglaze cobalt blue after the Turkish Iznik style were exported to Britain. Sir Christopher Wren became interested in the style of Ottoman

Jahangir holds a picture of the Madonna in this Mogul miniature of 1620. Jahangir, who had a reputation for being a connoisseur, is thought to have lacked any deep religious convictions.

William Hodges was an accomplished artist who visited India in 1777 and travelled widely, making many drawings of monuments and landscape. He left in 1783 and back in London published his *Select Views of India*. Two sepia aquatints are shown here.

Top: The mosque at Gazipoor. Hodges noted what he termed 'its great singularity', especially in relation to the minarets.

Bottom: A gateway to the mosque at Chunar Gur, a fort on the Ganges where Hodges spent a month with Warren Hastings on an expedition against Raja Chet Singh. In a note he asserts his belief in the common Muslim ancestry of Mogul and European Gothic architecture.

Below: A design by Johann Heinrich Müntz for a building in Kew Gardens which was known as the 'Alhambra', although its only links with the original are the proportions of the arcading and the use of colour. The drawing is dated 1750.

domes when he was engaged in finalizing the designs for St Paul's Cathedral, and he used his contacts with the Levant Company to obtain detailed information on the domes of Istanbul, including those of Hagia Sophia. The structure of the numerous saucer domes in the aisles and other parts of St Paul's Cathedral is believed to have been based on this research.

But it was not until the mid-eighteenth century that the idea of erecting a complete building in an exotic style took shape. In 1750 the Prince of Wales commissioned Johann Müntz to prepare a design for a building in the 'old Moorish Taste' to be erected in Kew Gardens. This building was known as the 'Alhambra' and was built in 1758 by Sir William Chambers after he had become both tutor and architect to the Prince. The design survives, but the two-storey building with a continuous balcony and colonnade has been demolished. It is quite unlike the original Alhambra, although Müntz is supposed to have visited Spain. A 'mosque' in the Turkish manner was also designed and built by Chambers at Kew and this has similarly disappeared, unlike the famous contemporary Chinese Pagoda. The designs for the mosque, and probably for the pagoda, were adapted from plates of buildings in the Arab, Turkish, Persian, Siamese, Chinese and Japanese traditions illustrating the third book of the history of architecture written by Fischer von Erlach, the Austrian architect who designed the domed Karlskirche in Vienna. Von Erlach's book was translated into English in 1737 and a Turkish tent based on one of the illustrations was erected in Vauxhall Gardens in 1744. The

Above: Thomas and William Daniell, uncle and nephew, travelled throughout India from 1785 to 1794. Between 1795 and 1808 they produced *Oriental Scenery*, a book of aquatint engravings. This is an example, a view of the mosque at Pillibead.

buildings at Kew set a fashion for garden pavilions and other structures in exotic styles. A typical example is the Moorish summerhouse built for William Beckford in his garden at 20 Lansdowne Crescent, Bath. Beckford was a wealthy scholar who had read *The Arabian Nights* in the original Arabic, written *Vathek; An Arabian Tale* in 1782 and visited Spain in 1785. He moved to Bath after dwindling finances forced him to sell his Gothic mansion, Fonthill Abbey, where he had fitted up his bedroom in the Turkish style.

The growing interest in the culture of the Near East was now supplemented by a parallel interest in the Indian sub-continent. William Hodges, an artist and writer, toured India observing and drawing all that held his interest. He had an eye for the picturesque and was fascinated by the scenery and the architecture, both Hindu and Muslim, showing his curiosity about the women's quarters of the palaces, which are strictly forbidden to strangers. On one occasion he accompanied Warren Hastings, the Governor, on a tour of inspection and was subsequently commissioned by him to

Right: Humphry Repton, the landscape architect and master of the Picturesque, was influenced by the work of Hodges and the Daniells as this view of his landscape scheme for the Royal Pavilion indicates. It is one of a dozen drawings submitted in 1808 to the Prince Regent. Eight years later, however, John Nash was appointed architect for the Pavilion.

Below right: A general view of the Royal Pavilion, Brighton, from the garden side. The interior of this exotic Mogul-style building was nevertheless decorated with Chinese wallpapers and other elements.

produce a number of oil paintings. He also visited the Taj Mahal, which filled him with wonder and admiration. After describing the use of white and coloured marbles, he wrote:

> the whole together appears like a most perfect pearl on an azure ground. The effect is such as, I confess, I never experienced from any work of art. The fine materials, the beautiful forms, and the symmetry of the whole, with the judicious choice of situation, far surpasses anything I ever beheld.

Hodges returned to England in the late 1780s and published travel books illustrated with aquatints, as well as a *Dissertation on the Prototypes of Architecture* (1786). The prototypes included buildings in the Moorish, Hindu, Egyptian and Gothic styles. In his commentary, he spoke against the prevailing admiration for Greek architecture as the model of perfection by whose rules all other forms are to be judged and condemned. He proposed the view that architecture should vary in accordance with climate, available materials and differences in social culture. Different styles of architecture should be judged on their own merits.

Another artist, Thomas Daniell, and his nephew William travelled extensively in India and painted many street scenes and landscapes, depicting the architecture with a painstaking attention to detail.

Their tour lasted from 1785 to 1794 and they assembled a huge collection of drawings and paintings. On their return to England they set about producing oil paintings and published volumes of engravings based on their collection. The most influential of these, comprising 144 aquatint engravings, was entitled *Oriental Scenery*. The Daniells' work was very successful and provided complementary picturesque images for readers of the contemporary Romantic poets and writers. Views of the Taj Mahal were particularly popular.

Inevitably these engravings were used as the basis for the design of exotic garden-set buildings. The most important building project on which Thomas Daniell's personal advice was sought was

The interior of the Royal Stables at Brighton, which were designed for the Prince Regent by William Porden. This building was completed in 1808. The Prince Regent was very pleased with its elegance and the animated effect of light and shade.

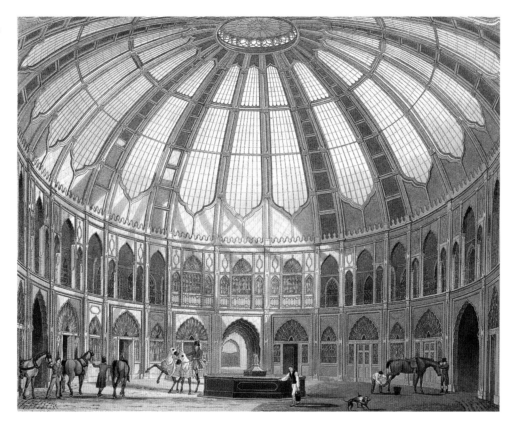

Sezincote House, in Gloucestershire, which was designed by Samuel Pepys Cockerell, Sir Charles's younger brother, then Surveyor to East India House. It was built between 1805 and 1810 as a residence for Sir Charles Cockerell, who had made a fortune in India and wished to introduce what he had admired there to the English countryside. This desire for exoticism was limited to the outside elevations of all the buildings, except the dairy, which was said to be Moorish in character. Thomas Daniell designed a bridge and a temple. The general effect of the main house and landscape was Mogul in character, emphasized by the onion dome and the carefully carved details of the house. The design of the interior was classical, however, with no hint of the Orient.

A few years previously, the Prince Regent had decided to build new stables and a new riding house in Brighton, where he had already built a classical villa to the designs of Henry Holland. The Prince Regent had fled London society because of his extensive debts and had settled in Brighton with his mistress, Mrs Fitzherbert. He had chosen Brighton because of the reputed healing properties of seawater (he was seeking a cure for his gout) and because it was also in reasonably easy reach of London. He commissioned William Porden to design the stables in an exotic style, probably inspired by a design that Porden, who had worked in Cockerell's office, had exhibited at the Royal Academy. This was entitled 'a Place of Public Amusement, in the style of Mahometan Architec-

Overleaf: An etching by John Martin of Sezincote House in Gloucestershire, which was designed by Samuel Pepys Cockerell for his elder brother Sir Charles Cockerell. It is one of ten etchings made in 1817 about a decade after the house's completion. Cockerell was inspired by the Daniells' renderings of Mogul buildings but, except for the conservatory in the left foreground, the interiors were all decorated in classical style.

The Senate House of the University of Madras (1879) was designed in the 'Indo-Saracenic' style by the British architect Robert Chisholm.

ture in Hindostan'. The stables, now known as the Dome and used as a concert hall, consist of a huge domed rotunda 65 feet high with windows and openings similar in detail to those of the Great Mosque at Delhi, as illustrated in an engraving published by the Daniells. The surrounding two-storey structure consisted of 44 stables for the horses at ground-floor level and harness rooms and living accommodation on the floor above. The Prince was presumably pleased with the new quarters for his Arab stallions, as his taste for the exotic was to develop with an even greater degree of fantasy. Because the new stables now overshadowed the villa in size and scale, he was determined to find the financial means to enlarge the villa and thereby redress the balance.

Interior designs for what was to be known as the Royal Pavilion were prepared for him by Porden not in the Mogul but in the Chinese style, possibly because the Prince had received as a gift a collection of Chinese wallpapers. (Apparently the Chinese style was considered to be too trivial for

large-scale English exterior design.) Meanwhile, Humphry Repton was asked to design the gardens in a Mogul style. In 1808 Repton submitted a portfolio of twelve watercolours showing the Royal Pavilion, an aviary and a pheasantry also in Mogul style. Decoration of the interior of the villa in the Chinese manner had been completed. It was not for another eight years that finance for the project was obtained and John Nash was appointed architect and commissioned to prepare designs for the pavilion. Eventually, a fantastic pleasure dome emerged. The total exotic exterior effect was achieved with a predominance of Mogul forms blended with a suggestion of Gothic. There is an assortment of eccentric onion domes and numerous slim minaret-like towers, while the veranda is formed by trellis screens pierced by pointed multi-foil arched openings. The exuberant interior, with its vivid use of bright colours, has a hectic medley of Chinese decoration within a classically planned framework. When the Royal Pavilion was completed in 1815, it created great interest and excitement but did not immediately set off a fashion for such eccentric buildings.

Indeed, the accession of Victoria to the throne in 1837 led to a general sense of disapproval of the frivolity of the Regency period. In India, although the British representatives of the East India Company appreciated the subcontinent's literary culture, the local architecture was not highly regarded. All new public buildings in India were in Georgian classical style, presumably to symbolize the distinction and the power of the newcomers. This attitude did not change until the demise of the Company after the Indian Mutiny (as it was called by the British), when the colonial civil servants began to consider themselves not merely as foreign conquerors but almost as indigenous. This change in attitude coincided with the expulsion of

A night view of the dome over the entrance to the palace of the Maharajah of Mysore. The palace was designed by Henry Irwin in an eclectic mix of Indian styles in which the Mogul predominated. The Maharajah was famous for his extravagant entertainments.

the last of the Mogul kings and the quest for a more suitable architectural style.

It is not surprising that the structural elements of the Mogul style (the dome and the arch) were found preferable to the Hindu forms with beams and flat roofs which could not easily be adapted to the larger spaces required for public buildings. A Mogul style, referred to as 'Saracenic', was proposed by some senior members of the Government for adoption as the official style. One of these was Lord Napier and when he was appointed Governor of Madras he promoted Saracenic designs for all public buildings. Ironically, the population of Madras in South India is predominantly Hindu, although the area had been occupied by the Moguls for a period. There are two prominent

examples of Saracenic architecture on the sea front at Madras. One is the University Senate House, built to designs by Robert Chisholm and completed in 1879. Its capacious hall, now used for examinations, has soaring arches over large windows with coloured glass panels. The other, more spectacular example is the vast complex of courts, offices, arcaded verandas and open stairways which was completed in 1892 by Henry Irwin and known as the Law Courts.

A large part of British India consisted of princely states and most of the princes built themselves lavish palaces for the reception of important guests. These palaces were designed in the European, Islamic or Hindu style or a mixture of all three. One of the most remarkable palaces was

The oil painting entitled *The Women of Algiers* that Delacroix exhibited at the Salon of Paris in 1834. It was developed from one of the watercolours made on his travels. The women portrayed here, except for the servant, were all Jewish since Delacroix would not have been allowed inside a harem.

designed by Irwin for the Maharajah of Mysore in South India. It is a huge complex in a hybrid style derived from that of palaces in Delhi, Agra and Rajputana in the north. The interior consisted of some halls in a stately European manner but the *pièce de résistance* is the Durbar Hall, which has an extravagant mixture of Hindu and Mogul elements, including stained glass with arabesque and peacock patterns. The source of the design principles of these developments was a monumental study, *The History of Indian and Eastern Architecture* (1876), which was written by James Fergusson after nearly forty years of measurement and observation. During the 1860s, using a new technique of photography in a comprehensive manner, the Government of India had also initiated the Archeological Survey in order to make an accurate record of the Indian cultural heritage.

Almost simultaneously with the disappearance of the last traces of Mudéjar architecture in Spain, a revival of interest in the heritage of the age of '*convivencia*' occurred. At the instigation of two scholars, Bayer and Casiri, the Spanish government commissioned the Royal Academy of Saint Ferdinand to send two architects under the direction of a captain of engineers to make measured drawings of the palace of the Alhambra in Granada and the mosque in Cordoba. In 1780 *Antigüedades Arabes de España* was published in Madrid, a volume which contained sixteen plates of Moorish design. It attracted the attention of scholars outside Spain and created a growing interest in these buildings.

Opposite: General Bonaparte during his short visit to Cairo at the time of the French occupation of Egypt (1798–1802). In the background are the Tombs of the Mamlouk Caliphs. The portrait was painted by Gérôme in 1863.

An interior view of the Hall of the Ambassadors in the Alhambra. This engraving appears in James Murphy's *Arabian Antiquities of Spain* (1813–15).

An Irishman, James Cavanagh Murphy, had been asked to travel to Portugal to make measured drawings of the church and monastery at Batalha. These drawings, published in 1795, reveal evidence of Moorish influence and are believed to have influenced Beckford in his design of Fonthill Abbey. Murphy then made a second journey to the Iberian peninsula. He landed at Cadiz in 1802 and travelled through Andalusia to Granada, where he was granted permission to enter the Alhambra whenever he wished. He later moved on to Cordoba, where he measured the mosque and the bridge. He stayed in Spain until 1809, when he travelled to London to prepare his drawings for publication. They appeared in 1815, the year after his death. Murphy's engravings give an impression of accuracy of detail but he employed a number of artists to produce them and they were later severely criticized by experts for their superficiality. In his *Handbook for Travellers in Spain* (1846) Richard Ford maintains that they were badly copied from the earlier Spanish volume. This last comment would seem to be unfair as Murphy's work contains ninety-seven plates, including perspectives, plans, sections, elevations and numerous details of the Alhambra, the Generalife and the Casa de Carbón, a courtyard house in Granada. Whatever their degree of accuracy, the plates are attractive.

Murphy was the forerunner of many scholars, architects and artists from western Europe and the USA who were fascinated by the sumptuous decoration and human scale of the Alhambra and of other Spanish buildings in the Moorish tradition. The end of the Peninsular Wars against Napoleon brought better access for travellers, many of whom had heard descriptions and stories from officers

and soldiers who had been deeply impressed by a society and environment very different from their own. In particular, the uninhibited flamenco music and the dances of the gipsies appealed to those with a taste for the exotic.

In France, Napoleon's short occupation of Egypt in 1798 provided the opportunity for a group of scholars and engineers to gather material for a thorough and comprehensive study of the Egyptian heritage, both Pharaonic and Islamic. This material was published in several volumes over the period 1809–29 under the title of *Description de L'Egypte*. Detailed drawings of buildings in the Pharaonic and Islamic styles opened up a new source of inspiration quite different from the strict classical tradition derived from Greek and Roman precedent. In 1832 the French painter Eugène Delacroix made a visit to Morocco in the company of a diplomat who had been instructed by Louis-Philippe to establish relations with the Sultan. Delacroix produced a collection of lively and colourful watercolours of the landscape and street scenes as well as a number of remarkable scenes of domestic interiors. The latter showed women in the family quarters which, according to Islamic custom, are out of bounds to any male who is not a close relative. This element of forbidden sensual delights was to become a feature of many Orientalist paintings, which remained much sought-after for the rest of the century. Delacroix's female figures were modelled on women at Jewish weddings to which he had been invited. He and the diplomat were eventually received by the Sultan at his palace at Meknes. The magnificence of the occasion so impressed Delacroix that, on his return to France, he used his sketches of the

A watercolour from a page in Delacroix's sketchbook that he completed during his visit to Morocco and Algeria in 1832.

Opposite: Six details of carved capitals selected from Owen Jones's *Plans, Elevations, Sections and Details of the Alhambra* of 1845. These were the first coloured plates of the Alhambra to be published and had been developed from the fieldwork of Owen Jones and Jules Goury.

Right: A portrait of Owen Jones painted by Henry Wyndham Phillips in 1857. It was commissioned by the Royal Institute of British Architects who awarded Jones their Gold Medal a decade later. He is standing in front of wall decorations from the Alhambra.

scene for oil paintings. The most famous painting to result from this trip is *The Women of Algiers*, which was exhibited at the 1834 Salon in Paris (and is now in the Louvre). His return journey was via Tangier, Andalusia, Oran and Algiers, where he spent only three days, though long enough to make sketches of Algerian women at their domestic tasks. In these sketches Delacroix rendered the sensuous beauty of the women, who were again Jewish, and their brilliant surroundings with an interlacing use of colours which to a certain extent anticipated the Impressionists. The odalisques of Matisse were later to repeat the subject matter of Delacroix. But it is the latter's watercolour depictions of Moorish scenes that convey, to use his own words, 'the living and vibrant sublimity that walks the streets here and whose reality completely overwhelms you'.

Another significant event took place in 1832. Owen Jones, a British architect, met Jules Goury in Egypt and they decided to travel together to Spain, via Constantinople, to visit Granada. Goury, a French architect, had previously accompanied Gottfried Semper, a German architect, on a tour of Greece, where they had both become especially interested in the polychromatic aspects of Greek temple design. (Most Greek Revival enthusiasts of the time had assumed that the temples had always been white.) It was because of Goury's particular interest in the use of bright colours by Islamic designers that he was attracted to the Alhambra, where there was then still some evidence of the original colours on a more extensive scale than the few surviving coloured fragments from Greek temples. Many of the colours at the Alhambra had faded through the passage of time but the richness of the decoration and the presence of primary colours, even in their faded state, must still have been a revelation. (It should be remembered that

Murphy's plates had not been coloured.) Both Goury and Jones deduced that the grounds of much of the decoration had originally been blue; the composition of the paint was metallic and through the process of oxidization it had been transformed to green. They then set out to make their surveys and colour analyses in preparation for publication. In 1834, however, Goury tragically

The main interior of the Crystal Palace at the 1851 Great Exhibition in Hyde Park, as depicted by William Simpson. This picture shows Owen Jones's proposed colour scheme, which was based on principles gleaned from his study of the Alhambra.

died of cholera in Granada. Jones took his body to France and then returned to England determined to publish their drawings in colour. He faced difficulties because no English printer had yet proved himself capable of mastering the skills of the new technique of colour lithography. He therefore decided to set up his own presses and hire draughtsmen and craftsmen direct. Jones was obliged to return to Granada in 1837 to revise some of the original drawings and to measure new subjects. At last, in 1845, two volumes were completed for publication. Four years previously, Richard Brown's volume on *Domestic Architecture* had been published. It included an illustration of

After the Crystal Palace had been reconstructed on a new site at Sydenham in 1854, a number of courts were created in different decorative styles. Owen Jones designed the Alhambra Court using features from the Court of Lions.

what was described as 'a Palatial Building in the Morisco-Spanish style' which was supposed to have been based on the Alhambra, although it featured a central pointed dome.

Jones had become fascinated by the Islamic use of colour and pattern and decided to study this in greater depth. In England, the use of excessive decoration had succeeded the relatively restrained taste for the classical. A W Pugin, in his promotion of the Gothic style, argued in his influential book *Contrasts* (1836) that decoration should grow out of the context. Jones supported this contention. He turned his attention to the design of wallpaper, textiles and geometrically pat-

Indian arts and crafts on display in the Crystal Palace in 1851. They were much admired by John Ruskin and others.

plain red, and a third painted with stripes of red, yellow and blue separated with narrow lines of white. The third scheme was finally chosen by Prince Albert and the Royal Commissioners, as Jones had hoped, but there was much initial opposition to this idea. The primary colours involved were similar to those at the Alhambra, while the use of the white lines followed the principles proposed by Michel-Eugène Chevreul, a French colour theorist, who maintained that they were necessary to keep the 'distinctiveness' of the primaries. Jones's ideas were also influenced by the Islamic approach to the use of colour in architecture, for example, the *cuerda seca* type of glazed tile decoration. A rendering by William Simpson in the collection of the Victoria and Albert Museum shows Jones's colour scheme for the interior of the Crystal Palace.

terned tiles, as well as to several interior design schemes for wealthy clients. It was probably his skill at using colour and pattern in his interior schemes that led to his appointment as one of the Superintendents of Works for the building, later known as the Crystal Palace, in which the Great Exhibition was to take place in 1851. He was appointed just after the construction of Joseph Paxton's pioneer design in cast iron, timber and glass had commenced in Hyde Park. Jones prepared details for the building, including iron railings in a Moorish type of fretwork, but his most important contribution was the colour scheme for the interior. The choice of colours became a matter of controversy, as Jones discovered after seeking the opinions of twenty architects. He decided to test three different possibilities on the cast iron columns; one group with a neutral tint, another

Jones explained the thinking behind his proposals for the Crystal Palace in a lecture he gave at the Royal Institute of British Architects. Stating that the colours emphasized the elegance of the structure and of the cast iron columns in particular, he put forward his proposition that, 'Construction should be decorated. Decoration should never be constructed.' After the Exhibition, Owen Jones was employed as one of the two Directors of Decoration under the supervision of Sir Joseph Paxton for the re-erection of the building on an open site at Sydenham. A series of courts illustrating historical decorative styles was constructed within the building, and Jones insisted that one should represent Moorish design. It was modelled on the Court of the Lions at the Alhambra and was completed in 1854. His supervision of the decorations, executed in what he believed to be an authentic manner, allowed thousands of visitors to experience some of the visual wonders of the Alhambra without travelling to Spain.

Jones also prepared designs for the Indian, Chinese and Japanese interior courts of the new South Kensington Museum. Sir Henry Cole, who had been the prime mover behind the Great Exhibition, was later to devote himself to the establishment of the museums in South Kensington as well as to the foundation of a number of schools of design throughout Britain. The Great Exhibition had contained an international cornucopia of design ideas, including a host of exhibits from India which had been much admired by John Ruskin, who later declared that Indian work was almost inimitable, observing that 'the love of subtle design seems universal in the race, and is developed in every implement that they shape, and every building that they raise'.

Yet Ruskin also disapproved of design if it was bound to the service of luxury and idolatry, though, like many others of his time, he confused morality and aesthetics in many of his artistic judgments. Cole initiated a special Indian collection at the newly opened South Kensington Museum and the import of Indian carpets and textiles increased as a result. Indian design, in the shape of the Kashmiri shawl which was woven in workshops in Scotland, had already influenced fashion in Britain. The main pattern element was based on a type of arabesque which has subsequently become known as the paisley pattern. It has been popular in textile design ever since.

However, most of the exhibits from Europe and the USA were the result of the indiscriminate reproduction by machine of past ideas. The contrast between the relatively simple structure of the Crystal Palace and the elaborate vulgarity of the majority of the exhibits it contained was only too evident. Cole was, therefore, convinced that industry was in need of trained designers to improve the quality of manufactured goods.

Schools of design were consequently established and were in need of suitable textbooks. Cole appears to have encouraged Jones to produce his celebrated pattern book, *The Grammar of Ornament*, for the use of design students, especially those who did not have direct access to the exhibits in what is now known as the Victoria and Albert Museum. This book was published in 1856 and the 100 beautifully coloured plates were introduced with a statement of 'General Principles in the Arrangement of Form and Colour, in Architecture and the Decorative Arts, which are advocated throughout this Work'. There are thirty-seven propositions which relate to general form, surface

Design for a printed cotton textile from a pattern book of Lockett and Crossland of Manchester issued in 1883. It features a unique use of the Moorish style for railway carriages.

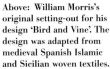

Above: William Morris's original setting-out for his design 'Bird and Vine'. The design was adapted from medieval Spanish Islamic and Sicilian woven textiles.

Above right: Plate 99 in the chapter entitled 'Leaves from Nature' from Owen Jones's *Grammar of Ornament*. This plate embodies the honeysuckle and the convolvulus. Christopher Dresser drew many of the plates in this chapter.

decoration, proportion, harmony and contrast, Oriental practice, the conventionality of natural forms, colour, the proportions by which harmony in colouring is produced, the contrasts and harmonious equivalents of tones, shades and hues, the positions the several colours should occupy, the law of simultaneous contrasts of colours derived from Chevreul, the means of increasing the harmonious effects of juxtaposed colours, observations derived from a consideration of Oriental practice and finally, imitations of materials. The worthy Victorian tone of optimism is set by Proposition 37, which reads: 'No improvement can take place in the Art of the present generation until all classes, Artists, Manufacturers, and the Public, are better educated in Art, and the existence of general principles is more fully recognised'. The plates are arranged with written comment in twenty

chapters relating to the ornament of 'Savage Tribes, Egypt, Assyria and Persia, Greece, Pompeii, the Romans, Arabia, Turkey, Moresque ornament from the Alhambra, Persia (Islamic), India, the Hindoos, the Celts, the Mediaeval era, the Renaissance, the Elizabethan era, Italy and leaves and flowers from Nature'.

The Grammar of Ornament was widely read by the design reformers of the late nineteenth century, including William Morris, who was known to have owned a copy. Indeed Morris used the repeat turn-over pattern found in medieval Spanish woven textiles in a fabric he designed and named 'Bird and Vine'; he gave the name 'Granada' to a silk velvet woven in three colours and brocaded with gilt thread. Christopher Dresser, a designer later celebrated for the silverware he designed in Art Nouveau style, had a special interest in botany. He had contributed a plate to *The Grammar of Ornament* showing the geometrical arrangement of natural flowers. There is, therefore, a continuous link from the rediscovery of the Alhambra at the end of the eighteenth century via the Arts and Crafts Movement to the Art Nouveau style at the beginning of the twentieth. Dresser acknowledged the great influence of Jones and advocated the study of Islamic design. Referring to some of Jones's buildings, he wrote:

> the excellency of these works calls loudly to us as a nation to do honour to Mr Owen Jones, who created them. I would that the nation should use him more while they have him; when it is too late we shall mourn our folly.

A prophetic comment, as only two of Jones's executed works survive today. Both are in London: a Moorish billiard room at 12 Kensington Palace Gardens and a decorative scheme at 16 Carlton

Opposite: A ceiling paper designed by William Morris. The design is called 'Persian'. It is composed of floral arabesques and is intended to achieve equilibrium as, according to Owen Jones, a ceiling design should have no direction.

House Terrace, which includes a ceiling with a Spanish *artesonado* geometric pattern. There is a remaining perspective of a design for a People's Palace (Alexandra Palace) to be built at Muswell Hill, London, in an Islamicized version of the Crystal Palace. There are also drawings by Jones of a similar scheme for an exhibition at a site at St Cloud, in Paris. Neither of these projects was realized. A coloured interior perspective of an unsuccessful competition design for a building for *The Manchester Art Treasures Exhibition* also survives.

Of the buildings Jones designed that were actually constructed the most important was St James's Hall in Piccadilly, London, on a site which the Piccadilly Hotel has occupied since 1905. It was completed in 1858 and was the most important concert hall in London for at least forty years. The complex, sponsored by the music publishers Chappell and Cremer, contained a great hall with 2,500 seats and two smaller halls, plus a restaurant and attendant kitchens. According to Helen Henschel, the concert hall had perfect acoustics and a unique atmosphere of intimacy and charm. It is hard to imagine a better recommendation for a concert hall. It was celebrated in its day and such prominent musicians as the violinist Joachim and the pianist Clara Schumann performed there. A perspective from the *Illustrated London News* shows an interior with a kind of Neo-Gothic treatment to a semicircular ceiling in the form of lozenge-shaped panels created by gilt ribs against a red ground. This colourful interior was given the adjective 'Alhambran'. It was suggested, however, that Jones had neglected certain practical considerations. The smaller halls below the main hall could not be used simultaneously with the upper hall without the sound of one concert interfering with the other. Smells from the kitchens were sometimes perceptible during performances and some claimed that the seating was cramped and uncomfortable. Intimacy and cramped seating were the positive and negative aspects of a more concentrated use of space than would be tolerated today.

Another hall used for the performance of music in London, albeit music of a more popular character, was built in 1854 on a site in Leicester Square. It was originally intended for exhibitions and was named the Panopticon. Four years later, the company that had built it went bankrupt and the hall was sold, converted for musical and theatrical shows and renamed the Alhambra. This name was considered appropriate because the original promoters had chosen its Saracenic or Moorish style as a novelty. The original design by T Hayter Lewis, based on an illustration of a Cairo mosque, consisted of a large rotunda with two main galleries facing a proscenium. The whole was surmounted by a glazed dome. The building had elaborate Moorish detailing, both internally and externally. In 1860, after an even more colourful and ornate redecoration, it became the Royal Alhambra Palace Music Hall. After a fire destroyed everything except for the front wall, the internal columns and the horseshoe arches in 1882, it was immediately rebuilt with the same popular medley of Moorish features and continued in its function very successfully until 1936 when it was replaced by a cinema. The Alhambra set a fashion for a number of Victorian music hall interiors in a variety of exotic styles; the process was known as 'Orientalizing'.

The impressive exterior of the Royal Panopticon of Science and Art in Leicester Square, London, as depicted in the *Illustrated London News* of January 1852 with its dome and two minaret-type pinnacles.

The galleried interior
of the Panopticon which
was described in the
Illustrated London News
in 1852 as a model of
Moorish grandeur that
was, at the same time,
no servile copy of any
existing edifice. The
illustration is from *The
Builder* of March 1854.

The Turkish bath continued to be popular among the urban middle classes and several new establishments were built at Jermyn Street, London, and in Manchester and Leeds. The Turkish baths in Leeds designed by Cuthbert Brodrick and demolished in 1969, had a powerful external articulation in multicoloured brick and stone with a series of domes surmounted with a pseudo-minaret. A prestigious private baths club with a more modest exterior was built in Dean Village, Edinburgh, to the designs of John J Burnet in 1882. It is known as Drumsheugh Baths and at one time contained a suite of Turkish baths with a dome supported on a brick and stone structure with simple Moorish details. The original club continues to occupy the building, although the Turkish baths and changing rooms, which were originally lit by antique Turkish lamps, now have timber flooring and are used as a gymnasium. The single-storey facade incorporates an elegant Moorish arcade with iron grilles in geometric patterns. The entrance hall has a window in a geometric Moorish style. The building is at the top level of a steeply sloping site. The main space is the swimming pool, which is at the lowest level and is reached by a staircase from the entrance via an intermediate level. The pool has many Moorish features, including brick and stone horseshoe arcades along the two long sides, supported on cast iron pillars and capitals. At the intermediate level, where the changing cubicles once were, there remains part of a timber screen with a design derived from the *mashrabiyya*. From here one can look down into the pool area. The inter-relationship between the interior spaces and the proportions of the Moorish detailing has been sensitively handled. The use of

Right: The West Pier at Brighton was built between 1863 and 1866 to the designs of Eusebius Birch. It was no doubt inspired by the Royal Pavilion and initiated a vogue for seaside piers in what was perceived as an Oriental style. The photograph was taken at the height of its popularity in the 1920s.

Below: A French Wagons-Lits poster and timetable featuring a similar pier in the Mediterranean.

tiles with black horizontal lines at the edges. There is a very limited use of plain blue-green glazed tiles in the former Turkish bath area.

There are Turkish baths in the Moorish style still in daily use in Dunfermline, Scotland, birthplace of Andrew Carnegie, the American steel magnate and philanthropist. The baths, called the Turkish Suite, are part of the Carnegie Centre, a building designed by an Edinburgh architect, Hyppolyte Jean Blanc, and completed in 1905 with financial aid from Carnegie. It replaced public baths that had been donated by him in 1877. The rich and colourful interior of the Turkish Suite is in total contrast to the dull grey stone exterior of the building, which is in Classical Revival style. The walls are decorated with polychrome glazed tiles in which blue and green predominate. The Moor-

colour is restrained, relying on the natural colours of brick and stone. Applied colour is mainly black and buff. The pool is lined with plain white glazed

ish theme is emphasized by the use of horseshoe arches at openings and niches, as well as a proliferation of traditional curvilinear patterns. This exuberant use of colour and pattern makes an interesting comparison with Burnet's restrained interiors at Drumsheugh.

It would be wrong to give the impression that admiration for the Alhambra and for Moorish design in general was accepted without opposition or criticism. Ruskin was at the height of his fame and influence in the 1850s and, although he did not disapprove of Islamic architecture in principle, he considered the Alhambra to be 'detestable... and its ornamentation is fit for nothing but to be transferred to patterns of carpets and bindings of books, together with their marbling and mottling and other mechanical recommendations'. Obvi-

ously his passionate hatred for the machine seems to have overwhelmed his judgment. Ruskin does not appear to have been consistent in his disapproval of the style he termed Oriental, for he admired the work of the painter John Frederick Lewis, who had made the Oriental tour. Lewis started in Spain, where he was overwhelmed by the beauty of Cordoba and the Alhambra, and continued to the Near East before settling in Cairo for ten years. Here he was visited by William Makepeace Thackeray, who described him at home there, living like an Oriental pasha in a splendid courtyard house. Lewis received Thackeray seated on a divan in the hall of audience. Opposite was another divan in the niche of a great bay window overlooking a garden, which contained a shrubbery with a great palm tree and

A painting of two young ladies relaxing at the Drumsheugh Baths in Edinburgh in front of geometric lattice windows framed with horseshoe arches. The baths were designed by John J Burnet in 1882.

Opposite: A view of the Arab Hall at Leighton House, looking towards the large window with its *mashrabiyya*-type latticework.

Below right: The architect's section through the Arab Hall at Leighton House, London. Designed by George Aitchison, the Hall was built in 1877–9. The decoration to the alcove in the west wall and the gold dome above are rendered in vivid colours for his eminent painter client.

a fountain. Thackeray made much of seeing two enormous beautiful black eyes watching him through the *mashrabiyya* as he walked across the court and records that Lewis assured him that their owner was only the black cook who had prepared the pilaf. On his return to England after his marriage, Lewis settled down to exhibit his considerable collection of watercolours which illustrated picturesque scenes of landscapes, streetscapes and interiors of Spain and the Near East. It was then that Ruskin claimed him as a Pre-Raphaelite because of his radiant use of colour, while acknowledging that he had been working in that manner long before Pre-Raphaelitism had been thought of. Ruskin also encouraged him to work in oils. This he did until the end of his life, mainly producing large versions of his watercolours.

Yet another English painter, Frederick, later Lord Leighton, became a collector of Oriental ceramics which he acquired on his travels. Eventually his collection grew to such an extent that it presented a storage problem at his new studio at Leighton House, Holland Park Road, London. Leighton then asked his friend, the architect George Aitchison, to design an extension as a setting for the collection. This room, known as the Arab Hall, was attached to the west side of the studio-house. It rises through two storeys with a dome above a pool and fountain at ground level. A *mashrabiyya*-type window lights the wide landing of the main staircase at first-floor level. From here one can look down into the hall below, as if from the family quarters of a genuine Arab house. The dome is perforated with small windows of stained glass, some of which were brought from Damascus. William de Morgan, the prominent ceramicist, was responsible for arranging the tiles in the hall, which were mainly Syrian and Iznik, dating from the sixteenth and seventeenth centuries. Many

of the sets were incomplete and de Morgan devised some ingenious infilling. There is also a mosaic frieze designed by Walter Crane in the Persian manner, while the main staircase has plaques of Turkish Eyoubi tiles within surrounds of tiles made by de Morgan, whose work was strongly influenced by the Iznik and Spanish-Islamic traditions of ceramics and is in harmony with the total effect. An inscription in Arabic on the stairs reads:

> This house has obtained cheerfulness
> And earned joy for the helpers,
> Written in prosperity on its doors.
> Enter it with peace, being safe.

An even more exotic interior, also known as the Arab Hall, was created at the same time by William Burges, a friend of Aitchison, at Cardiff Castle, a huge Neo-Gothic castle built for the Marquess of Bute, who was a wealthy landowner. Burges used the full repertoire of Moorish design, including stalactite vaults, *mashrabiyya* and Kufic inscriptions. A great variety of iridescent materials, including crystal, glass mosaic and lapis lazuli, give an impression of glittering luxury. Burges was aware of the work of Owen Jones but it appears that the immediate source of his detailing was a French publication, *L'Art Arabe d'après les monuments du Kaire*, by Prisse d'Avennes.

In France the increasing contact with the Islamic world following colonial activity in Algeria, Morocco and Tunisia had encouraged the study of Islamic design and architecture.

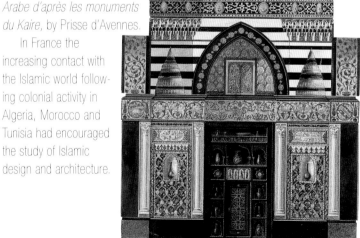

Jules Bourgoin produced a study of the Arab decorative arts. Joseph Brocard, a glassmaker, revived the Syrian technique of enamelling on glass. He made imitation mosque lamps in the style of the thirteenth and fourteenth centuries. These, together with some original Islamic pieces, were shown at the Paris Universal Exhibition of 1867. Emile Gallé, the outstanding glassmaker from Nancy, admired Brocard's work and was also inspired by Venetian and Islamic prototypes. In 1871 he travelled to London to study the examples of Oriental glass in the South Kensington Museum. He later developed new colour techniques and special effects but always based his designs on patterns from nature, especially flowers and plants. He became the most celebrated Art Nouveau designer in glass.

In Germany, meanwhile, Karl Zanth, who had studied both Greek and Islamic polychromatic ornament in Sicily, had designed the Villa Wilhelma in a Moorish style for the king of Württemberg in 1837. The villa, associated with an open-air theatre and casino, was sited near his palace on the banks of the river Neckar near Stuttgart. Another German monarch who enjoyed fantastic surroundings was Ludwig II of Bavaria. At first, he favoured romantic Gothic castles. Later, he chose an elaborate French Rococo style for another castle at Linderhof, near Garmisch, but incorporated what was curiously termed a Moorish Kiosk containing a Peacock Throne. Three magnificent peacocks in colourfully enamelled cast bronze and false precious stones are set about the throne, one above and behind it and one on either side. Ludwig was an admirer and patron of Richard Wagner. Might he have been dreaming of some exotic music drama when he commissioned it?

Gottfried Semper, the architect who gave practical, three-dimensional form to Wagner's dream of an ideal opera house at Bayreuth, had been Goury's companion in the earlier study of Greek polychromy. Like Wagner, Semper had been involved in the 1848 revolution and had consequently been forced to leave Germany, eventually settling in Switzerland. He was the outstanding

Left: A panel of enamelled tiles by William de Morgan dating from 1896. De Morgan was much influenced by the design of Turkish Iznik tiles and assisted Frederick Leighton with the arrangement of the ceramic panels in the Arab Hall at his studio house in London.

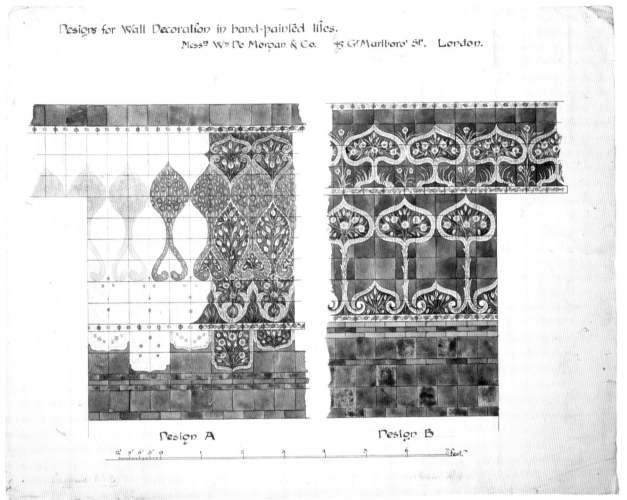

Designs for Wall Decoration in hand-painted tiles.
Messrs W^m De Morgan & Co.   45 G^t Marlboro' S^t.   London.

Design A

Design B

Left: Two original 'Persian' designs for wall decoration in hand-painted ceramic tiles by William de Morgan, dating from 1890.

Overleaf left: The Moorish interior of the Villa Wilhelma near Stuttgart which was designed by Karl Zanth for King Wilhelm I of Württemberg as a private retreat. It was inaugurated in 1846 for the wedding of the King's son. The story at the time was that Zanth had used Owen Jones's work on the Alhambra as a source for his detailing.

Overleaf right: William Burges designed the Arab Room at Cardiff Castle for the Marquess of Bute in 1880. The elaborate polychrome ceiling is centred on an octagonal star supported on four bracketed sections composed of a series of faceted stalactites. Burges studied Islamic architecture closely and was indebted to the drawings of Prisse d'Avennes.

German architect of his time and usually favoured a Renaissance expression to his functional planning. He believed and taught that functional form should be modified in a way that related to tradition and the existing social order, 'the symbolic form'. However, in 1839 he had designed a synagogue in Dresden in what was to become the Moorish Revival style. Although this pioneering building had a plain Romanesque-style exterior, the interior was elaborately decorated with polychromatic stucco, carved wood and ceramics.

This combination of styles presumably met the demands of tradition and existing social order.

The synagogue predated two important Spanish publications. The first was *Toledo Pintoresco* by Amador de los Ríos, published in Madrid in 1845, which contained a detailed description of the former synagogue, Santa María la Blanca. The second, which came out in 1857, was the *Historia de los Templos de España* by Gustavo Adolfo Bécquer, which also contained descriptions both of Santa María la Blanca and of the Tránsito

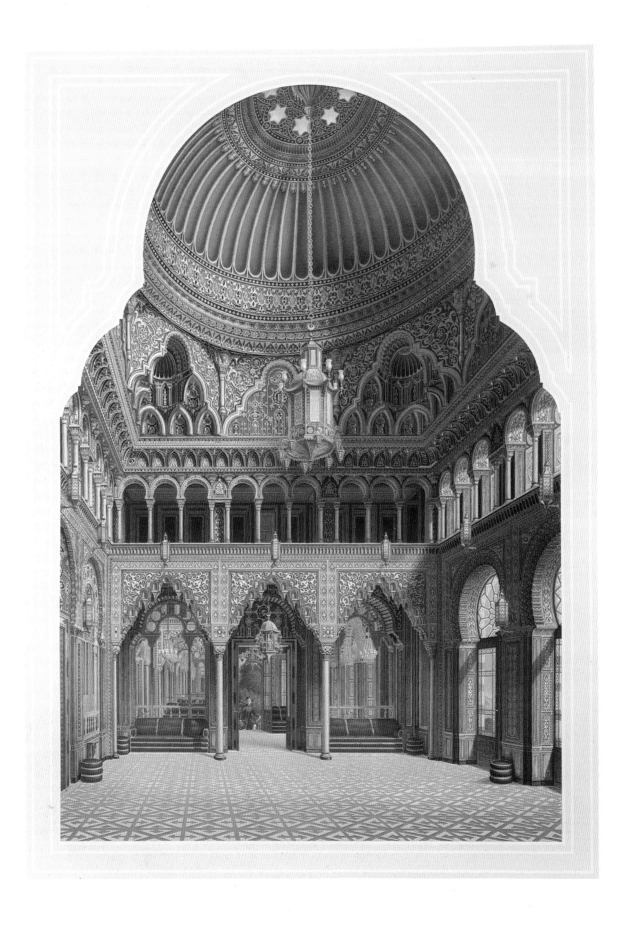

Above: The dome over the main entrance spaces and a pinnacle of the Berlin synagogue, as seen from the street.

Right: The sectional drawing by the architect, Edward Knoblauch, who died before the completion of the synagogue.

synagogue in Toledo. A year earlier, an important article on the Tránsito by Heinrich Graetz had appeared in the *Monat-schrift für Geschichte und Wissenschaft des Judenthums*. These, and other, publications spread an increasing awareness of the Judaic culture of the Spanish caliphate and its significance both for the Jews and European culture in general. It therefore seemed appropriate to many Jewish scholars and architects to equate a Spanish-Moorish style of architecture with Jewish spiritual and aesthetic values, especially as there was a lack of information on the architectural character of the ancient synagogues. The success and growing confidence of the Jewish community in Germany and Austria-Hungary encouraged the building of new synagogues in a style distinct from the dominant Gothic character of Christian churches. Segregation was abolished and the 'enlightened' Jewish communities of Vienna and Berlin played significant roles in the cultural and business life of those cities. Semper's example of a Romanesque exterior with a Moorish interior became a popular solution since it combined a non-Gothic external form, which had no obviously provocative iconography, with an interior which created a more identifiably Jewish atmosphere.

A more integrated Moorish Revival style was adopted by Otto Simonson in his design for a synagogue in Leipzig. Simonson had studied architecture with Semper and believed that Moorish architecture was a legitimate external expression of Jewish spiritual values. Two new synagogues in a similar style were constructed to designs prepared by Ludwig von Förster, a professor at the Academy of Architecture at Vienna. The one at Budapest had the largest seating capacity of any synagogue in Europe, with space for 1,492

men and a three-sided gallery to accommodate 1,472 women, but the most prominent features were the twin minaret-like onion-domed towers. The popularity of the full-blooded style increased, in spite of strongly voiced opposition in the writings of Albrecht Rosengarten, who preferred a straightforward use of the Romanesque with a Byzantine plan.

In the early 1860s a spacious synagogue with a bulbous dome and elaborate Moorish detailing was built in Berlin to the design of Edward Knoblauch. Berlin's Jewish community, which was then the largest in Germany, was divided into two main groups: Orthodox and Liberal. The latter needed a new building for their 20,000-strong congregation. The existing synagogue that they had already rebuilt in classical style had become too small for their needs. They decided that a new building should accommodate 1,400 men and 800 women. Two sites were considered. One, offered by the King of Prussia, was an expansive site, though some distance from the city centre, where most of the congregation lived; the other was nearer the centre and in an area where many Jews lived but it was difficult and narrow. After much discussion the second site, in Oranienburg-erstrasse, was chosen and an architectural competition held to settle who should design the building. In the event, the jury decided that none

of the designs submitted was suitable for the difficult site, which was not only narrow but at an angle to the main street where the entrance was to be. It was also enclosed by neighbouring buildings on both of its long sides. The chairman of the jury, the Berlin architect Edward Knoblauch, was then asked to prepare a design. This he was reluctant to do because of the restrictions imposed by the site but he was eventually persuaded to proceed. He planned the main space of the synagogue as a long rectangle following the long axis of the site and set at an angle to the generous entrance hall on the street frontage. It was lit from above through five glazed cupolas and included galleried seating accommodation for women on three sides at first-floor level. An early interior perspective shows a relatively simple treatment with a coffered

Below: The synagogue built in the early 1870s at S Rumbach utca in Budapest was an early work by Otto Wagner, the celebrated architect of the Viennese Secession. This three-dimensional sectional drawing by Wagner shows the lofty octagonal space of the prayer hall and the entrance hall, with the ancillary spaces above. Part of the street facade, with its minaret-like towers, is also visible.

The main facade of the Via Farmi synagogue (1874–82) in Florence. Designed by Falcini, Micheli and Treves, it was built in the Moorish Revival style with some Byzantine overtones.

lower levels. As for the exterior, the cupolas over the temple were not visible from the street; great emphasis was therefore given to the entrance, where the hall was taken up through three storeys and surmounted with a tall onion dome above an octagonal drum. The main dome was flanked by two lantern towers topped with smaller domes. The entire street elevation was decorated with elaborate Moorish details and the domes were finished with gilt ribs in a tracery of flowing curves. Construction started in 1859 but Knoblauch died before the completion. The building of the interior was supervised by August Stuler, who also died before the synagogue was dedicated in 1866. The exact details of the colourful interior are not known as only a part of the complex remains after extensive damage sustained during World War II.

Moorish exoticism continued to be a feature of synagogue design in Austria-Hungary. Another example in Budapest, an early work by the Viennese architect Otto Wagner, who had worked for von Förster, was the synagogue at S Rumbach utca, built in 1872–75. Its Moorish character was emphasized by two minaret-like towers. It was a sensitive and refined design with all the expected elements of Moorish interior decoration, including carved stucco patterns and coloured ceramics carefully integrated with the structure in a way that Owen Jones would surely have approved of. This principle was applied later in the work of the Viennese Secession, of which Wagner was a member, but the character of the decorative elements was to change. The human figure was introduced as an important component of the overall design.

Jewish communities in other European countries were also to embrace the Moorish Revival in the design of their synagogues. One of the most interesting is to be found in the Via Farmi, Florence. It was financed from the estate of a promi-

ceiling but in the event it was built with lavish ornamentation in the Moorish style. A report in *Die Vossische Zeitung*, a newspaper of the time, reads:

> The light streams through the coloured glass, magically subdued and transfigured. Ceilings, walls, columns, arches and windows have been extravagantly decorated and form, with their gilding and decoration, a wonderful wreath of arabesques which is wound into a harmonic whole of fairy-like and supernatural effect.

The dados and holy shrine were of marble: while yellow and gold were predominant on the higher surfaces and blue was the main colour at the nent Florentine, David Levi, and was built over the period 1874–82 after the demolition of the ghetto. It is attributed to three designers, Mariano Falcini, Vincenzo Micheli and Mauro Treves. The plan is Byzantine, with a central dome after that of Hagia Sophia but there is extensive use of the horseshoe arch in the external elevations and a very elegant and rich use of Moorish decorative elements inside.

An Italian marchese shared King Ludwig's fascination with the exotic and the peacock motif in particular. He enjoyed the resounding title of Marchese Ferdinando Panciatichi Ximenes d'Aragona. His ancestors, under the name Ximenes d'Aragona, had acquired the Villa di Sanmezzano at Rignano sull'Arno, near Florence, in 1605. The villa passed by inheritance to Panciatichi in 1816. By 1853 Marchese Ferdinando had initiated a series of alterations and additions which transformed the villa into a palace worthy of the tales of Scheherazade. The Hall of Peacocks is in a hybrid style derived from the Moorish tradition and the florid Spanish version of Gothic known as Plateresque. The form of the peacock's tail is expressed in the elaborate carving of the fanvaulted stucco ceiling. The peacock motif is also suggested in the design of a doorway which has a horseshoe architrave in carved stucco combined with an original treatment of arabesques. In contrast, the dado is decorated with polychrome glazed tiles in dynamic patterns. The Marchese's motivation for surrounding himself with a Moorish style of decoration, in a way that accommodates the Western way of life, seems to stem from pride in his Spanish ancestry. An inscription in Italian on the wall of the octagonal White Hall reads: 'Proud blood of Aragon runs in my veins'. In the entrance vestibule the family motto '*Non plus ultra*' appears in gold over the horseshoe arch at the doorway.

These extensive internal works continued until 1873 when, merging the roles of client and designer, the Marchese started to develop the exterior of the villa and its parkland setting. The park was already planted with many exotic species, including palms, giant sequoias and cedars of

A close-up of the ornate Moorish interior arcade of the Florentine synagogue with a side gallery above.

Lebanon. He designed a new gatehouse and in 1889 completed a central entrance porch with a tower set with mini onion-shaped domes at each corner and incorporating a tall pointed multi-lobed arch with a large clockface above it. An elaborate parapet wall with merlons was also thrown around the entire villa. All the external walls are decorated in relief with horizontal linear patterns marking the storeys, as well as lozenge motifs between the second-floor windows. Except for the entrance tower, the exterior lacks the conviction and vitality of the interior spaces.

The nineteenth century was the great era of emigration from Europe to the USA. It was inevitable that ideas from Europe should have influence both among new immigrants and those who had long been established in a huge country that was in a state of rapid evolution. One of the latter was Washington Irving, an American of British Protestant descent who had literary ambitions and who came to Europe in 1815. He based himself in London, travelled to Germany, Austria and Italy, then became friendly with the US ambassador to Spain, who offered him a post at the American Embassy in Madrid. There he developed a long-lived passion for the history and culture of Spain and began to write a lengthy history of the life and voyages of Christopher Columbus. He discovered the picturesque charms of Andalusia, spending a year in Seville, followed by another in Granada, where the Governor granted him the use of three rooms in the Alhambra. In 1829 he wrote:

Opposite: A detail of the polychrome cupolas that decorate the ark of the Princes Road synagogue in Liverpool. This magnificent building was built in 1874 to the designs of W and G Audsley.

Right: A view of the main interior space of the Liverpool synagogue. Moorish and Byzantine elements, together with a rose window, combine to form an exuberant and eclectic mix of styles.

I tread haunted ground and am surrounded by romantic associations. From earliest boyhood when on the banks of the Hudson I first pored over the pages of an old Spanish story about the wars of Granada, that city has ever been a subject of my waking dreams, and often have

I trod in fancy the romantic halls of the Alhambra...As I loiter through these Oriental chambers and hear the murmur of fountains and the song of the nightingale, as I inhale the odour of the rose and feel the influence of the balmy climate, I am almost tempted to fancy myself in the paradise of Mahomet...

Above: A painting on ivory in the 'Company Style' showing the peacock throne of the Mogul emperor Shah Jehan. The painting dates from 1850.

Right: The fabulous Peacock Room at the Villa di Sanmezzano near Florence. The villa was owned by Marchese Ferdinando Panciatichi who carried out a series of internal transformations during the 1850s. Here the fan-shaped peacock's tail sets the theme for the stucco and ceramic decoration.

While there Irving listened to the stories of the many locals who lived in or near the palace. He wrote his history of Granada and made notes for his later famous work *Tales of the Alhambra*. He was then recalled to London, where he completed the romantic tales of love, war and buried Moorish treasure which were to become world-famous.

In the USA, these tales perpetuated the picturesque attraction of the Alhambra. Among those who were fascinated by them was Barnum, the successful showman. He decided to adopt an exotic approach to the building of his own residence near Bridgeport, Connecticut. This was a result both of his affection for Irving's writings and his admiration for the Brighton Pavilion, which he had visited. To a certain extent, the Pavilion influenced the details of the design, which was commissioned from Leopold Eidlitz, an architect who had emigrated from Prague to the USA. The three-storey building had a simpler plan and fewer onion domes than the Royal Pavilion but the

verandas were almost identical in design. It also had a Chinese library. Its very name was exotic: Iranistan. It was completed in 1848. By 1855 Barnum was bankrupt but, because his creditors were unable to sell Iranistan, presumably owing to its eccentric design, he was allowed to continue to occupy it. In 1857, however, the house was destroyed by fire – but it had already set the fashion for a number of prominent and rich citizens to express their taste for what was then called 'the Oriental' in their personal surroundings.

A Mississippi cotton planter, Dr Haller Nutt, visited Egypt. On his return he asked Samuel Sloan to design a mansion for him at Natchez. He chose Sloan as his architect because in 1852 Sloan had published a design for an 'Oriental Villa' in his book *The Model Architect*. This design was adapted for Nutt's mansion, called Longwood, which survives as a National Historic Landmark, although in an incomplete form. It has an unusual plan; a central rotunda is surrounded by four rectangular

Above: A more realistic interpretation of the peacock occurs in the Peacock Throne of King Ludwig II of Bavaria, which is situated in the Moorish Kiosk at Linderhof Castle. The three peacocks were made of enamelled cast bronze and fake precious stones by Le Blanc Granger of Paris while the throne was made in Munich by Anton Püssenbacher in 1877.

Top: An imitation glass mosque lamp by Philippe-Joseph Brocard decorated in enamel and gilt. Dated 1880, it was presumably intended for the adornment of the house of a wealthy connoisseur rather than for use in a mosque.

Bottom: Decorated with gold and enamel, this glass bowl of 1893 is the work of Fernand Thesmar of Paris.

rooms which are in turn encircled by four more rectangular rooms arranged on the diagonal at the junctions of the inner four rooms. The outer rooms are linked by verandas and an entrance porch. The main three storeys are thus expressed externally as an octagonal form. This is surmounted by a multi-faceted drum supporting a single pointed dome.

Frederick E Church, the painter, was a similar enthusiast for Moorish themes. He built his house, Olana, at Greendale in New York State, with the help of the architect Calvert Vaux. The studio wing contained decorative motifs copied directly from the Alhambra. Although eclecticism had become the norm in architectural design in the USA as in Europe, the use of the Moorish style was still relatively unusual for most types of building. The Farmers' and Exchange Bank at Charleston, South Carolina, had been designed by Francis D Lee with a front elevation in a Moorish Revival style. The ground-floor windows were surmounted by horseshoe arches and the first-floor windows had cusped semi-circular arches. There was also a commercial building in New York, the Tweedy Store, in which the architect, Richard Morris Hunt, used Moorish arches.

As in Europe, the type of building in the USA that was most likely to attract the Moorish approach to design was the synagogue. Many of the new immigrants practised Judaism and this created a demand for new places of worship. When Leopold Eidlitz, Barnum's architect, was commissioned to design the Emmanuel synagogue in New York, it seemed natural to him and his clients that he should adopt the approach that was dominant at that time in Austria-Hungary, where he and most of the congregation had originated. A few years previously in 1866, the Isaac M Wise temple had been built in Plum Street, Cincinnati, setting the future pattern. It was designed by James Keys Wilson and featured no less than thirteen domes and two towers in minaret style. Inside were slender pillars and other distinctive architectural details borrowed from the Alhambra. The Moorish Revival was to hold sway in American synagogue design until well into the twentieth century. Perhaps the most elaborate example was the Park East Zichron Ephraim synagogue at Lexington and Third Avenues in New York, built in 1889 for a reform congregation of German origin. A wealth of Moorish detail was used within a basilica-type plan arrangement.

The potential of the Moorish style to express a sense of occasion was similarly exploited for exhibitions, especially if they were international in scope. Such an example was the Horticultural Hall erected for the centennial celebrations of Philadelphia to the plans of Herman Schwartzmann. A later example was Louis Sullivan's Transportation Building for the Chicago World Fair of 1893. In the previous year Sullivan had been responsible for the Wainwright tomb, which had a distinctly Islamic form with a hemispherical dome over a cube decorated with a rectangular frame of geometric patterning. In all his work Sullivan showed great interest in pattern as a decorative medium but he always used it in a strictly disciplined way that never overwhelmed the formal expression of the structure. This skill in the use of pattern in a variety of forms was inherited by Frank Lloyd Wright and many other American architects and designers. The exotic aspects of eclecticism by now ranged well beyond the Moorish, Persian, Indian and Chinese to incorporate Japanese and Pre-Columbian traditions in the use of pattern and colour in all the visual arts. The beginnings of a style of expression that could be seen to be more than a mere rearrangement of elements copied directly from both the past and from exotic contemporary cultures began to emerge in the USA as in Europe. Influences were now to flow in both directions across the Atlantic and the new style in decoration, architecture and fine art embodied to a greater or lesser degree all these exotic elements. For example, Louis Tiffany, the American glass and jewellery designer, had met and was influenced by William Morris and Emile Gallé. He also collected Oriental works of art, including many from Spain, North Africa and the Near East. He was acclaimed for achieving beautiful iridescent and lustre effects in blue, green, gold and pink in his glassware, which was sold on an international scale and influenced European designers. In his vases and jewellery he introduced natural flowing patterns and arabesques.

Carlo Bugatti, an outstanding Milanese furniture designer whose later work is regarded as being Art Nouveau in style, produced elaborate cabinets in Moorish style during the last two decades of the century. A typical example of this work incorporates finely detailed inlays of wood and metal decorating horseshoe-arched openings which vary in size and proportion. The plain flat surfaces of the cabinet are covered with vellum, a material that Bugatti later used to cover the entire surface of his furniture. Much of it assumed strange inflated forms, as in his so-called 'snail' room at the Turin International Exhibition of 1902. The vellum was painted and gilded with stylized

plant and insect motifs. When Bugatti exhibited at the Italian Exposition of 1888 held at Earl's Court in London, his furniture was described as 'quaint and in Moorish style' by critics writing in contemporary magazines. Some years later, Bugatti was commissioned by Lord Battersea to furnish his London home.

A cabinet and stand made from ebonized rosewood with inlays of brass, pewter and ivory. It was designed by Carlo Bugatti and dates from the turn of the century. The use of horseshoe arches was typical of Bugatti's work of this period and shows his affection for the Moorish style.

While elements of Moorish, Japanese and Chinese culture were being absorbed into a unified style which is generally referred to as Art Nouveau or Jugendstil, an architect in Barcelona was creating a series of remarkable buildings in an individual version of this hybrid style. To understand the work of Antoni Gaudí it is necessary to refer to the literary developments that occurred in Spain in the mid-nineteenth century. A taste for the picturesque was established when *Escenas Andaluzas* by Serafin Estébanez Calderón appeared in 1847. It was followed in 1849 by *La Gaviota* by Cecilia Boehl de Faber (under the pen name Fernan Caballero), which contained similar descriptions of Andalusian life and picturesque customs. This type of writing was dubbed *costumbrismo*; it was a form of realism based on local colour, especially that found in the environment of Andalusian towns and villages. Slowly, changes in literature affected the visual arts.

The Mudéjar tradition had survived to a limited extent in the vernacular architecture of Spain. It was recognizable in carpentry, patterned brickwork and some uses of ceramics and plasterwork where geometric pattern-making was still part of active craftsmanship. In the formal building sector where Gothic and French Renaissance reigned supreme, it had almost disappeared. There were a few exceptions. Rodriguez Ayuso's Bull Ring in Madrid, for example, was in a neo-Mudéjar style, with iron and steel used for the structure. This interesting building, since demolished, is known from photographs. Railway stations at Toledo and Seville also embodied the same combination of a metal structure and neo-Mudéjar details. However, in 1882, Rada Delgado, of the Academia de San Fernando de Madrid, declared that the architecture of the nineteenth century must be eclectic. This statement followed the claim by Victor Hugo and others that there must be liberty in art, which

implied that all cultures are worthy of study and that there should be freedom of choice in style. But earlier, in 1871, the Academy of Architecture in Barcelona had purchased an extensive collection of photographs of Oriental buildings which had inspired a revival of interest in the colour and liveliness of the Moorish and Mudéjar traditions.

This renewed interest coincided with the desire to find a new vocabulary of visual elements that could be used to express a newly industrialized society's need to be seen as modern and cosmopolitan. In the case of Barcelona the desire was reinforced by the rising pressure of Catalan Nationalism. Eusebi Guell, one of the most successful of the new industrialists, became Gaudí's most influential client. While he was working on the first commission from Guell Gaudí made an extensive tour through Andalusia and Morocco. Enthusiasm for the exotic now prevailed in the upper-class salons of Spain, and there is a recognizable use of Moorish and Mudéjar elements in Gaudí's early works. The Casa Vicens in Barcelona, a large house built for a brick and ceramics merchant, is

Far left: A lithograph by Sarony and Major of 'Iranistan', the home of the showman P T Barnum. It was built in 1846–8 at Bridgeport, Connecticut, to the designs of Leopold Eidlitz. Barnum's inspiration was Brighton Pavilion but his house has a simpler skyline and more emphasis on the vertical.

Left: During his travels through Palestine and Syria the painter Frederick Church developed a keen enthusiasm for Islamic tiling. Thus on his return to the USA in 1870 he decided to design and build, with the help of architect Calvert Vaux, a house in which to keep his collection of Islamic objets d'art. The house, which displays some Moorish detailing such as this corner tower, is named 'Olana' and situated at Greendale in New York state.

Above: The design of the timber latticework of the ticket office at the main railway station of Toledo shows the influence of *mashrabiyya* and Spanish *artesonado* skills.

Right: The corner tower and balconies of the Casa Vicens (1883) at Barcelona. This house, which was built for a brick and ceramics merchant, is an early work by the famous Catalan architect Antoni Gaudí. It demonstrates a completely original use of complex elements taken from the Moorish and Mudéjar traditions of Spain.

Opposite: Interior details of the Smoking Room in the Casa Vicens. A *muqarna* ceiling, the timber fretwork to the windows and the decoration to the glass lamps (based on Arabic calligraphy) make a rich and original composition of Moorish features.

an extravagant showcase for the client's wares. Outside there is a lavish use of geometric patterns of coloured ceramic tiles which contrast with rough brickwork and random stone. The colours and patterns become more dominant and bizarre the higher up the facade of this three-storey ornamental castle they go. At the roof line are several small towers of a distinct Moorish character. Corner balconies decorated with the same elaborate patterns of ceramic tiles as the towers protrude at the upper storeys. Inside, the decorative effects are even more overwhelming, achieved with the use of a galaxy of materials and a medley of stylistic precedents, including Art Nouveau. The smoking room is the space that has the most direct relation to the Moorish tradition, with its stalactite ceiling in stucco, coloured ceramic tile dado, geometrically patterned joinery and glass lamps with enamelled pseudo-Arabic calligraphy. At the same time that Casa Vicens was under construction, another house for a rich bachelor was being built near Santander. It is a two-storey structure on a sloping rural site and is known to the local people as El Capricho, which can be loosely translated as The Folly. Again the decorative emphasis is at the eaves line. The exterior patterning of brick and ceramic tiles with moulded flower motifs in horizontal lines, although complex, seems relatively restrained compared with Casa Vicens. The extravagance in this case is concentrated on a prominent non-functional cylindrical tower over the entrance porch. This has the form of a minaret and is decorated with ceramic tiles. Inside, the decorated timber ceilings owe much to the *artesonado* tradition.

A detail of the mosaic made from fragments of broken ceramic tiles, many of them with Moorish patterns, which was selected by Gaudí and applied to the back of a long, snake-like bench in Guell Park, Barcelona.

While Gaudí was developing his designs for Guell's city residence, he was also supervising the building of three pavilions on Guell's country estate. They consist of a porter's lodge and two pavilions linked together to form stables and a riding hall. Over the riding hall is a cupola and lantern in Moorish style. As the stables and riding hall are inward-looking, there are large plain areas of external wall; these are divided into decorative panels of brick and ceramics which are derived from the Mudéjar tradition, especially the perforated parapet walls. Gaudí's later work was more influenced by the Neo-Gothic style and Art Nouveau. Gaudí's individual, plastic approach to surfaces can be attributed to his potter ancestry. He welded these materials into a personal style but never lost his fascination for surfaces decorated with bright ceramic tiles, often used in a mosaic of broken pieces. One example is the brightly coloured finish to the curved surfaces of the endless outdoor bench in Guell Park. When at his most characteristic, he succeeded in creating a wonderful synthesis of surface, ornament, structure, space composition, light, colour and texture.

As to the New World, the skills and several features of the Moorish tradition are also to be found in some of the buildings created during the colonial period. It is not clear whether any of those who professed the non-Christian faiths found their way to what was later called America when the expansion of the Spanish Empire was initiated by Christopher Columbus in 1492, the year the Jews were expelled. The pressure and hostility against the Muslim inhabitants of Spain also increased under the Inquisition. The classical style was used by the Spanish to stamp a visual presence on the conquered peoples in the same way as the British did in India. The conquest of the Moors was compared with the conquest of the American Indians so the Conquistadores in the New World, unlike the British in India, had a strong religious mission in addition to their commercial motives, and parallels were drawn between the Reconquest of Moorish Spain and the conversion of the American Indians to Christianity. In the aftermath of the conquest the building of churches became a priority for them. There was a shortage of skilled craftsmen amongst the newcomers and the native population was unfamiliar with European forms of construction. The Spaniards introduced brick technology and the use of arches and vaulting. In Peru, there was a tradition of almost unbelievably precise stone-cutting and masonry but elsewhere local building methods depended on the use of what appeared to the Spaniards to be temporary materials unworthy of church building. It was necessary to set up craft schools, particularly in carpentry, which was a new skill to the indigenous people. A Carmelite brother in Mexico, Andres de

San Miguel, who became interested in architecture, published a book *Arte y Uso de Arquitectura* in which he described very clearly the principles of '*la carpintería de lo blanco*'. Where stone was in short supply, timber construction was considered suitable for hot climates and less liable to collapse in earthquake-prone areas. The carpentry was often based on these principles. Consequently, a large number of the early churches had *artesonado* ceilings, sometimes elaborately painted and gilded. One such example is the church of San Francisco in Quito, which has a combination of rib vaulting with a painted and gilded timber *artesonado* ceiling of some complexity. Another example of a fine ceiling, with evidence of Mudéjar precedent in its elaborate geometric patterning, is to be found in the church of San Francisco in Bogotá, Colombia.

Seville, which had a royal monopoly on trade with the New World, was the last city in Spain to be seen by the Spanish emigrants who brought with them a taste for richly decorated surfaces and the skills of polychrome plasterwork. The making and fixing of glazed tiles also travelled across the Atlantic. This is particularly evident in Mexico, where many large church buildings, often in the Baroque style, have all their plain surfaces decorated with ceramic tiles, both glazed and unglazed. The patterns used owe much to Moorish precedent, as does some of the stuccowork. Puebla became a centre for the ceramics industry and attracted many settlers from Andalusia. It is believed that potters were persuaded to come from Toledo to train local craftsmen and establish workshops. The dome of the cathedral at Puebla was faced with bright green and yellow glazed tiles and a similarly extensive use of brightly coloured ceramics can be seen on the church of Santa Catalina. Many prominent houses incorpo-

The colourful glass roof to the National Hotel in Mexico City was designed by the American craftsman, Louis Comfort Tiffany.

rated areas of ceramic tiling, externally and internally. The Casa del Alfeñique has a lavish use of panels covered with a pattern of unglazed tiles and *azulejos*. The taste for ceramic tiles spread to the capital, Mexico City; the large mansion now called La Casa de los Azulejos and the home of Sanborn's Restaurant was built in a blend of Mudéjar and Baroque. The use of colourful ceramic tiles as

wall panelling in a domestic context, especially in the kitchen, soon became commonplace. The ceramic industry still flourishes in Puebla.

Perhaps the most celebrated example of a secular building with Moorish features is the Palacio de Torre Tagle (now the Peruvian Foreign Ministry) in Lima, which was the colonial capital of Spanish South America. It was built in the early eighteenth century around a courtyard with foliated arches. At the first-floor level of the street elevation it has timber projecting balconies which are reminiscent of *mashrabiyya*; they have perforated timber screens to the windows, while the timber panels are carved and shaped in geometric patterns after the Mudéjar tradition. They must have found favour because an entire street of courtyard houses built in Lima during the second half of the nineteenth century has balconies of similar design. This was long after Peru won independence, when any artistic expression which could be connected with Spanish colonial power was unusual. Similar balconies feature on the main facades of the Archbishop's Palace and the City Hall of Lima, two prominent neo-Baroque buildings dating from the second quarter of the twentieth century.

The traditional skills of making and fixing *azulejos* and other forms of ceramics were active in Spain during the nineteenth century and it is believed that both craftsmen and tiles were brought from Spain to Santiago de Chile. In 1862 a mining magnate from Santiago wished to build his residence there in a style copied from the Alhambra. While it was still under construction he sold it to a government minister who brought Arabstyle furniture from Paris. The Palacio La Alhambra, as it was named, has two storeys and is planned around two courtyards, one of which is a reproduction of the Court of Lions. It is now used as an art gallery and cultural centre.

Opposite: The projecting timber balconies of the Archbishop's Palace in Lima, Peru, are reminiscent of *mashrabiyya* and derive from the Spanish Mudéjar tradition. Built in 1939–44, this palace was designed by Ricardo de la Jaxa Malachowski, an architect of Polish origin who was trained in Paris. He settled in Peru in 1911 and later became Government Architect.

Opposite: The moving diaphragms of the glass window walls to the Institute of the Arab World in Paris. They open or close automatically according to the strength of the daylight and are intended to be a modern form of the *mashrabiyya*. The building was designed by Nouvel, Lezènes and Soria.

Right: A print entitled *Allah Mohammed Ali* by the artist and architect Issam El-Said. He used square Kufic script to create a beautifully proportioned three-dimensional pattern based on the cube. It is dated 1975.

And how beguile you? Death has no repose
Warmer and deeper than that Orient sand
Which hides the beauty and bright faith of those
Who made the Golden Journey to Samarkand.
James Elroy Flecker

The arcaded Palacio Español laid out on a semi-circular plan at the Plaza España in Seville. It was built in 1929 as part of the complex of pavilions designed by Anibal González for the Spanish-American exhibition. The balustrade of the bridge in the foreground is encased in brightly coloured glazed ceramics in the Mudéjar tradition.

In the same way that Catalan nationalism was a factor in the development of Modernismo in the arts in Barcelona, so regional and national pride had led to the rediscovery of the Mudéjar tradition in Aragon. The municipal architect of Saragossa, Ricardo Magdalena, in his design for the Faculty of Medicine and Sciences of 1886, used many details that were derived from the Mudéjar style. This was particularly evident in his treatment of the brickwork. Magdalena thus established a precedent for a form of neo-Mudéjar in the design of public buildings. The new Central Market of Saragossa was opened at the turn of the century, a time when the country felt an emotional need to express some form of national identity because of

the loss of the last of its overseas colonies, the Philippines, Cuba and Puerto Rico. The Market displays a combination of cast and wrought iron with brick and stonework. Many of the decorative details reveal an awareness of Mudéjar forms (which is not surprising as the architect, Felix Navarro, originated from Teruel), although the structure and planning of the building are similar to contemporary French examples. The market building formed part of an urban design scheme that included new town residences in a similar style. The expansion of an iron and steel industry in Saragossa occurred simultaneously with the establishment of a school of arts and crafts there and the encouragement of craft skills in the build-

One of two bullrings in Barcelona, the Plaza de Toros Monumental was completed in 1915. The architects were Ignasi Mas and Joaquin Raspall. They appear to have been influenced both by the Mudéjar tradition and by the buildings of the Viennese Secession. The design is a vigorous mixture of the two styles with bold decoration in patterned brick and ceramic tiles.

Detail of the elaborate fretted decoration of the multi-lobed arches on the ground floor of the Museo de Artes y Costumbres Populares.

ing industry by the municipal architect and the new bourgeoisie. This led to the construction of a number of buildings with a rich repertoire of finely worked features in ironwork, carved stone and patterned brickwork. The influence of Catalan architects was evident, particularly in the swirling curves of the ironwork. One such example is the Casa Juncosa, a large residential building designed by Magdalena in a wide boulevard in a new residential area. Another, but a rather more modest, residential building in the same street is decorated externally at ground-floor level with chromatic patterned glazed ceramic tile insets in the brickwork. The architect, Luis de la Figuera, employed a series of horseshoe arches in a house nearby.

Magdalena was appointed architect in charge of a Franco-Spanish trade exhibition held in Saragossa in 1908, though he did not design all the pavilions. The only building to survive today is the bandstand, or *Kiosko para la Musica* as it is known in Spanish. This remarkable structure was re-erected in a public park and has an air of Art Nouveau and exoticism. It was designed by two brothers, José and Manuel de Ubago. They were born in Pamplona but José had been trained in Barcelona and Manuel in Madrid. Eight cast iron columns stand on an octagonal stone podium supporting a glazed roof of eight cantilevered fan-shaped sections. At the centre of the roof there is a dome of elliptical profile covered with colourful ceramic tiles. The structural framework is adorned with a medley of circles and curves which are both functional and decorative. Judging from photographs, the other exhibition buildings were not as festive in character but were more ornate, with elaborate stone carving of less elegant proportions combined with statuary.

The exhibition was followed by a decade of building in a stylistic mixture of Modernismo and regional eclecticism but the neo-Mudéjar predominated towards the end of that decade. The most notable proof of this is the main post office of Saragossa, which was designed by Rubio in 1917. It has a complicated street facade in brick with stone dressing. Above an arcaded ground floor there is a comparatively simple storey of rectangular window openings but the top two storeys have semi-circular arched openings with panels of brick tracery over them. Two arches on the top storey are of the horseshoe type. The facade from the first floor upwards is divided vertically into five sections. The central main section and the two outer sections project onto the street frontage and are surmounted by overhanging decorated brick eaves; the two remaining sections are set back. Elsewhere in Spain at this time, similar post offices were built in provincial capitals in a variety of

styles, usually relating to their local historic context. Neo-Mudéjar was the choice in Aragon and Andalusia, possibly because the Moorish cultural tradition was most evident in these provinces. This taste even extended to Latin America, where the main post office in Mexico City appeared in full-blooded neo-Mudéjar. The desire for some form of regional identity may have been the reason for the choice of this style in Spain and there may have been a symbolic association with the acquisition of Spanish Morocco. In Mexico the style would be associated with the country's former colonial power; nevertheless its use may have been a deliberate gesture of independence and solidarity with Spain, after the loss of yet more territory to Mexico's powerful northern neighbour.

From the 1920s onwards, rationalism in design began to predominate and soon any form of historicism was either confined to occasional details or was totally omitted. There were some exceptions in Spain after the Civil War, when references to tradition were approved by Government and Church. Teruel was such a case. It suffered considerable damage during the war. Not only were the historic Mudéjar buildings restored but much of the new construction was in neo-Mudéjar style. A prominent example is the public flight of steps known as the Escalinata. Here the full range of

The upper part of the facade of the Museo de Artes y Costumbres Populares in Seville shows three different types of arches. The building, which was formerly the Mudéjar Pavilion for the 1929 Exhibition, was clearly influenced by the fourteenth-century palace of the Alcázar in the same city.

brick and coloured ceramic patterning is expressed
in the balustrades, retaining walls and the symbolic
tower at the head of the stairway.

During the latter half of the nineteenth century,
the French extended their colonial domination over
North Africa, beginning with the invasion of Algeria
in 1830 and achieving total control by 1847.
The following year the French constitution granted
Algeria representation in the National Assembly.
During this period the French policy was one of
assimilation and there was much talk of a *mission
civilatrice*. After the military situation had been
stabilized, this mission was expressed by the construction of wide boulevards, often driven
through historic high-density urban centres
where Islamic religious endowments were
declared to be obstacles to development. The boulevards were lined
with large-scale neo-classical buildings very similar in style to Hauss-
mann's developments in Paris. For
the French in Algeria, like the British
in India, the new style became a
tangible expression of victory and of
the superiority of the newcomers.
The coastal towns expanded rapidly
with the opening-up of trade with

France. New residential areas, at a much lower
density, were constructed for the incoming traders
and settlers behind a neutral zone designed
to separate them from the original inhabitants
of the old settlements, like the Casbah of Algiers.
The lower part of the Casbah was taken over for
commercial purposes and dominated by European
traders. The remainder was neglected.

This policy, however, was opposed by
many intellectuals in France, among whom was
Théophile Gautier. Eventually an official change
of policy was announced by Napoleon III on a visit
to Algeria in 1865. He declared that he was as
much Emperor of the Arabs as of the French and
stressed that greater respect should be paid to
long-established local traditions. The new policy
was termed *association*. When the French took
over Tunisia in 1881, they declared it to be a protectorate. This meant that Medina, the historic city,
was preserved but its development was hindered
by the rigid layout of the new quarters. In 1867
a Universal Exhibition was held in Paris at which
picturesque exhibits from all the African colonies
were displayed. At the second Universal Exhibition
in 1889, the Palais Algérien contained a partial
reproduction of a sanctuary and a Moorish café,
while the Palais Tunisien incorporated a replica

Top: The interior of the spectacular Palace of Mirrors at the 1900 Paris Exhibition, showing Emile Hénard's liberal use of large multi-lobed arches and *muqarnas* on the surfaces of the domed ceilings.

Bottom: A general exterior view of the Porte Binet, showing the dome and the large multi-lobed arches. This gate, situated in the Place de la Concorde, was the main entrance to the Exhibition.

The voluptuous figure of the *Woman of Algiers* was painted by Auguste Renoir in 1870 as a tribute to Delacroix. The model was Lise, his usual model, dressed in Oriental clothing. Renoir's first visit to Algeria took place eleven years later.

sanctuary designed by Henri Saladin, who had been responsible for a thorough study of Tunisian arts and architecture. Three years later, a rich industrialist called Vaissier built himself a large château in Moorish style at Tourcoing in northern France. Similarly, the impressive interior of the Palace of Mirrors at the Paris Universal Exhibition of 1900 was designed in an extravagant version of Moorish style.

Overseas meanwhile, the concept of *Arabisance* was promoted. It was to inspire the introduction of 'Arab' decorative details to buildings which were often basically neo-classical in concept. This trend occurred originally in Algeria and later in Tunisia and Morocco. It was also seen in Cairo, where rich Europeans and local princes introduced elaborate Moorish details to their new luxurious villas. But it was not until the first decade of the twentieth century that this change in attitude affected official policy in the design of public buildings. Two important public buildings in Cairo were constructed in what was perceived to be a neo-Arabic style: the Museum of Arab Antiquities

and the Ministry of Waqfs (Religious Endowments), designed by Mahmoud Fahmy Pasha.

Preferential treatment had always been given to European traders in Morocco and this led to the eventual occupation of the country by Spain and France. In 1912 the Spanish took over a zone to the north, which included Tangier and Tetuan, while the French administered the larger remaining zone as a protectorate, with Rabat as their seat of residence. Jonnart, the governor of Algeria, and Marshal Lyautey, the new governor of French Morocco, gave their support to the neo-Moorish style, an acknowledgement that the excellence of traditional Islamic style was worthy of emulation. Henri Prost, who had won a competition for the preservation of historic Antwerp a few years previously, was put in charge of physical planning. He was assisted by an architect, Albert Laprade, who studied in great detail the total environment of the medina of Rabat as well as of Salé, the historical port and former home of the Andalusian corsairs. He then sought to combine the advantages of a modern technical infrastructure with the social rel-

Odalisque in Red Trousers was painted by Henri Matisse in the Orientalist tradition in 1921, nine years after the last of his two visits to Morocco. A western model lounges in front of a background of Moorish tiles.

evance of Moorish interior courtyards, also incorporating neo-Moorish details and decoration. The new medina at Casablanca, which embodied these principles, was only partly successful, in that the wealthy local merchants who could afford to do so preferred to live in villas like their European counterparts. A number of public buildings were built in Casablanca in a neo-Moorish style during the period of the Protectorate and among them is the city hall, where there is a series of courtyards and richly decorated interiors. More unexpected are the Cathedral of the Sacred Heart and the Archbishop's Palace in Algiers. The encouragement of the use of traditional Moorish decorative elements rejuvenated traditional Moroccan arts and crafts which would otherwise probably have disappeared. The skills of Moroccan craftsmen consequently survived the pressures of modernization and are now in demand throughout the Middle East.

French painters continued to be interested in North Africa. In *Woman of Algiers*, which he exhibited in 1870, Renoir had used what were then known as Orientalist themes. An exhibition entitled *Exposition d'Art Musulman* was presented in Paris in 1893 and this was claimed to be the first major exhibition devoted solely to Islamic art. Soon after, the *Société des Peintres Orientalistes* was established and Orientalist painting became fashionable in France. Henri Matisse visited Algeria in 1906 and again six years later, when he also travelled through Morocco and Andalusia. As a result of his travels he painted colourful versions of a Moroccan garden and a scene in Tangier, and later his celebrated series of *Odalisques*.

Wassily Kandinsky, a painter of Russian origin, visited Algeria and Tunisia in 1904. He was deeply impressed by the visual environment, the powerful effect of light and colour and the lack of figurative

Left: A striking water-colour by the German painter, August Macke. Entitled *Kairouan I*, it was painted in 1914 when he visited Tunisia in the company of Paul Klee.

Opposite: Paul Klee painted this watercolour, *Red and White Domes*, in 1914. The picture shows Klee's interest in colour grids which he was to develop later at the Bauhaus as a result of his fascination with Islamic mosaics and ceramics. He was to return to the theme of Kairouan on many later occasions.

art. In 1910 he produced his first wholly abstract watercolour. In the same year he joined Der Blaue Reiter group in Munich. Here another exhibition devoted to Islamic art was held, which both Matisse and Kandinsky visited. Kandinsky was to join the staff of the Bauhaus when it was established under the direction of Walter Gropius after World War I. Paul Klee, another painter who was later to become a colleague of Kandinsky at the Bauhaus, had also settled in Munich before the war. In 1914, in the company of August Macke, he spent several weeks in Tunisia. This visit was to be the turning point in Klee's development as a colourist. Over the next twenty years he was to return regularly to the theme of Qairouan,

Hammamet and other places he had seen in Tunisia. At the Bauhaus, he developed a series of abstract colour exercises based on square grids. In these studies he created mosaics of subtle colour impressions with a wider range than that of the ceramics, in primary and secondary colours, that formed part of the built environment of Tunisia and had become embedded in his visual memory. Later, in 1928, Klee was to write in his diary: 'Mosques of Qairouan show indeed that Tunisia is purer. In comparison, the Cairo mosques are kitsch, practically all of them, even those with two stars in Baedeker. On the other hand, the whole confusion here of Europe-Orient Africa is simply stupefying in its magnificence.'

Arabian Nights

Top: The title page of Lady Burton's edition of her husband's *Arabian Nights* (1886), translated from the Arabic. This edition has been further edited for 'household reading'.

Bottom: A scene from the musical film of 1933, *The 1,002nd Night*. The designers have clearly used their imagination with the extravagant Moorish motifs in the scenery and costumes.

Across the Atlantic, the USA was in the throes of rapid industrialization and associated economic growth. Many businessmen had benefited from this process. Some of them were now so wealthy that they were able to indulge themselves by constructing their fantasies in three dimensions, following the example of Barnum in the late nineteenth century. Inspiration came from reading the tales of Washington Irving and translations of *The Arabian Nights* or viewing Hollywood films. One of the richest and most celebrated American magnates of the time was John D Rockefeller, whose smoking room was decorated in consistently luxuriant Moorish style. (It is preserved in the Brooklyn Museum, New York.) A yet more fantastic manifestation appeared later in Florida, in a district called Opa Locka in the northern suburbs of Miami. It is claimed that, within its 4^1/$_2$ square miles, the district contains the USA's greatest concentration of Moorish Revival architecture. About seventy of the original buildings are still standing. Here Glenn Curtiss, a land speculator who had previously made a fortune building aircraft for the US navy, was able to combine the creation of a fantasy world with the making of money. He built this development in the 1920s after seeing the film of *A Thousand and One Nights*. He obtained a copy of the book and instructed his architect, Bernhardt Muller, to base his designs on the illustrations, which may have

been reproductions of the vivid watercolours by Edmund Dulac that first appeared in 1907. The city hall appears to be a Westerner's idea of a mosque with an informal arrangement of several minarets, domes and courtyards. Even the mayor adopts Arab dress for special occasions. A variety of imitation Moorish details are distributed throughout a haphazard composition that has the air of a film set in the round. A number of houses built on standard ranch-type floor plans sport Moorish details selected from a stock of features that includes domes, tall minaret-like chimneys, castellated rooflines, horseshoe arches and so on. The town was not completed before the onset of the great Depression, but it made a good recovery afterwards. It has, however, suffered recently from

One of Edmund Dulac's illustrations for *The Stories from the Arabian Nights*, dated 1907. It carries the quotation: 'He arrived within sight of a palace of shining marble.' These illustrations were the source of inspiration for Glenn Curtiss's development at Miami which was built during the 1920s.

Overleaf: The main facade of the City Hall at Opa Locka, a suburb of Miami designed by Bernhardt Muller for Glenn Curtiss, the developer. The informal assembly of Moorish themes is reminiscent of a film set.

A night view of part of the Country Club Plaza district of Kansas City. The development of what was then an out-of-town area started in the 1920s. According to the developers, the district represents 'a blend of Old Spain, Mexico and Southern California'.

urban decline, poverty and racial tension. Yet, the power of Curtiss's fantasy lives on because newcomers are still drawn to settling there, in spite of the difficulties. A restoration programme is currently under way and it is hoped that the future will be a positive one.

Almost simultaneously, a pioneering exercise in community planning was taking place in Kansas City, the traditional testing ground for Hollywood movies. Jesse Nichols had founded a development company to construct a residential area which he called the Country Club District. In addition to generous plots for houses, he set aside land for schools, churches, parks and shopping centres. To gain inspiration for his commitment to excellence, he travelled extensively in Europe. He foresaw the age of the motor car and proposed to build a shopping area where the customers would arrive by car. This was the principle behind the layout of what was to be the Country Club Plaza. The word 'plaza' is significant since the precedent for Nichols's design style was Spanish or, to be more

specific, the city of Seville. On his European tour Nichols had been captivated by Seville and the predominance of colour, ornament, fountains and courtyards that he saw there. He wanted to create the same atmosphere in Kansas City, and was particularly keen on the use of coloured ceramics and ornamental ironwork. The style of this now extensive shopping centre is, in the developers' own words, 'a blend of old Spain, Mexico and Southern California'.

Twelve towers rise above the general roofline. The tallest is the Giralda Tower, a simplified and smaller version of the Giralda in Seville. Edward Delk prepared the master-plan and was the consultant for most of the early buildings of the Plaza. The Plaza Theatre, whose architect was Edward Tanner, has an ornate tower and an interior in the Spanish style, supplemented by a seventeenth-century door and doorway brought from Spain. The first suburban shopping centre in the USA to be designed specifically for the motorist has continued to expand with its commercial success, but the quality of the 'Spanish' design with many Moorish elements has not been maintained since Nichols's death in 1950. There is now a curious mixture of Moorish, Baroque and Modern. The layout is Baroque in scale and the fountains are accompanied with statuary in the Baroque manner, whereas the parking arrangements are essentially Modern, the layers of cars in the multi-storey car park hidden by screens of perforated brick and ceramic in Mudéjar style.

Both Curtiss and Nichols shared their Moorish fantasy with the general public and this was to their financial advantage. A kind of open-air theatre was introduced into the streetscape and, in the case of Curtiss, the spur was the cinema. The expansion of the cinema in the USA and Europe coincided with the decline of the attraction of historic eclecticism to architects and their clients. Both the cost of using elaborate details from past ages, and their symbolism, came under fierce attack. The Austrian architect Adolf Loos declared ornament to be a crime and the Modern Movement, as it was later called, began to extend its influence. The doctrine of functionalism led to the belief that anything that did not serve a structural or practical purpose should be omitted. This had the added advantage of economy at a time when the ravages of World War I had created an urgent need to produce a large number of buildings as quickly and as cheaply as possible. In this designers of theatres and cinemas faced a dilemma because their interiors were expected to create an atmosphere of occasion. It was difficult for them to do this without introducing some forms or features that were not strictly functional.

In 1919 Hans Poelzig was commissioned to remodel the Grosse Schauspielhaus in Berlin for Max Reinhardt, the famous theatrical producer. Poelzig used a profusion of stalactite shapes such as *muqarnas* which, with skilfully articulated coloured lighting, created a cave-like space that was compared at the time to an Oriental dream. This design was to influence the approach to cinema design in Britain in the 1930s. In Germany and Central Europe, cinemas were usually designed by architects of the Expressionist school who used bold curved and horizontal shapes. In the USA, however, a more historical approach informed the huge building programme which got into its stride between 1910 and 1920 and which continued into the next decade. The cinema was likened by the promoters to a 'palace of dreams'. To achieve an aura of enchantment, inspiration was sought from Mediterranean countries. Controlled lighting was an essential factor in the creation of the desired effect. In the most fantastic examples, the décor gave the illusion of being outdoors under a soft moonlit sky, with the screen and proscenium absorbed into an exotic palace or group of pavilions in a splendid garden. The extravagance of the design usually extended to the foyer and the exterior. The Moorish style was one of several eclectic styles used. One of the most successful designers was John Eberson, an engineer trained at the University of Vienna who had emigrated to the USA in 1901. Based in Chicago, he designed nearly 500 cinemas and specialized in this atmospheric approach. A typical example in Hispano-Moresque style was the Pitkin, which was built for Loew's in Brooklyn, New York. Another was the Tampa in Tampa, Florida, which sought to imitate a Spanish courtyard.

In Europe, the great cinema-building era was delayed by World War I. Many promoters in Britain followed the American pattern, though in a slightly more restrained fashion. As in the USA, a variety of styles was used. The Alhambra Theatre in London, which had been converted into a cinema,

Above: The first Odeon cinema at Perry Bar, Birmingham, which was designed by Stanley Griffiths and Horace Bradley and opened in 1930. The symmetrical elevation is in a simplified Moorish style but the Odeon chain later changed to their characteristic modern expressionist manner.

Right: The 'Fountain Court' at the Astoria cinema in Finsbury Park, London. This cinema was designed by Edward Stone in a strange mix of Moorish and Byzantine styles with a hint of Art Deco.

Opposite: The interior of the Grosse Schauspielhaus, Berlin, which was remodelled in 1919 by Hans Poelzig for the producer Max Reinhardt. The ceiling consisted of a blend of coloured lighting and a continuously flowing composition of *muqarnas* which created the impression of an Oriental dream.

inspired several designers to adopt the Moorish style of decoration. The Astoria at Finsbury Park, London, for example, was built to the designs of Edward Stone in a curious blend of Moorish and Byzantine, including a fountain court. Another smaller example was the Palace in Portsmouth, designed by A E Cogswell, which has an Indian-Moorish exterior complete with dome. It is in the tradition of seaside piers derived from the Brighton Pavilion.

John Eberson designed the Rex Cinema in Paris in what was called a Moroccan style, while the largest cinema in Australia, the State Cinema in Melbourne, was erected to his Moorish designs inside and out. The Granada Cinema chain in Britain employed a theatrical producer, Theodore Komisorjevsky, who had been trained as an architect in Russia, to design a number of their early cinemas. The interiors of the Granada, Dover, and the Granada, Walthamstow, were inspired by the Alhambra. But for his largest and most extravagant work, the Granada, Tooting, he turned to the Venetian Gothic. A rival chain, Odeon, also adopted a Moorish style for their first cinema, the Odeon, Perry Bar, Birmingham. The Odeon, Northfields, by Cecil Masey, which was known as 'Spanish City', was in a hybrid style, a mixture of Moorish and Baroque. The Odeon chain then changed to the modern German mode of design and adopted it as their corporate style.

World War II and the destruction that came in its wake once again brought an urgent need for building programmes in which utility and speed of erection were the priorities. There was no place

for fantasy and decoration was regarded as a waste of money, even in buildings for public entertainment. Such indulgence as was allowed was usually confined to planting, landscape and sculpture, applied or free-standing. Television now undermined the film industry and few cinemas were built. Churches were spartan in the approach to their external and internal design, the desire for beauty being partly satisfied by the installation of stained-glass windows. Even the economic expansion of the 1970s and 1980s produced few build-

ings in which the exercise of fantasy and luxury could persuade the majority of the public that contemporary buildings can be as beautiful as those of some golden age in the past. This seems to be the currently prevailing attitude in Western countries.

Structures intended to house the machinery used in industrial processes are normally made as simply and cheaply as possible. This is because the increasing speed of technological change means that such buildings tend to have a short lifespan. In the production of wines, however, traditional methods are often seen as a guarantee of quality. So when Pedro Domecq SA of Jerez de la Frontera, the long-established firm of sherry producers, needed to expand their storage capacity for the maturing of sherry in oak butts, they decided to build a long-life bodega, or warehouse, in a traditional Andalusian style. As there was a requirement to provide aisles for access to the rows of butts and no need for a large, clear roofspan, a traditional structure based on the Great Mosque of Cordoba with repeating columns and medium-span arches was selected by the designer, Javier Soto, who is a member of the Domecq family. (The founder of the family firm was a partner of John Ruskin's father, who was then their agent in England.) The bodega was completed in 1974, when the centenary of the first Spanish brandy was being celebrated. It covers nearly three hectares and is known locally as *La Mezquita* (The Mosque) because of the spatial character of its vast interior.

As to the Islamic world itself, the large-scale extraction of oil in the Near East has brought economic advantages to several Islamic countries and as a result the building industry has greatly expanded. There has been an increase in urbanization with the construction of low-density residential areas on the perimeter of older settlements and the development of new commercial and

industrial zones. This has been accompanied by the building of many new mosques and other religious facilities. The style of the new secular buildings has usually been in a modern international vein that has little or no relevance to the local culture, climate or way of life. Most of the houses have been built using modern materials in a way that demands wasteful mechanical air-conditioning and negates the environmental advantages of the traditional courtyard house. Some exceptions exist where wealthy citizens have built large villas in a style that attempts to create an appropriate cultural identity. Mosques, on the other hand, have always been designed in such a way that they are instantly recognizable and obviously follow what is accepted as a correct historical style.

The Moroccan decorative style has changed little since the days of the Marinid dynasty in the fourteenth century, as Morocco escaped Ottoman occupation and during the French protectorate the traditional crafts were officially supported for use on public buildings. Since independence, King Hassan II has continued to promote this policy. The mausoleum of his father, Mohammed V, in Rabat, was built in a neo-Moorish style during the 1960s and was designed by an architect from Vietnam, Vo Toan. Within this complex of buildings, which is carefully related to the surviving minaret of the Almohad mosque of Hassan, there is a phenomenal demonstration of the full repertoire of Moroccan arts and crafts, including every conceivable combination of polychrome geometric and arabesque patterns in carved stucco, timber (mainly cedar), glass and ceramics.

Until its completion in 1993, hundreds of craftsmen were occupied with working on a huge new Great Mosque at Casablanca, large enough to accommodate 100,000 people at prayer. It is the first stage of a scheme to rebuild a consider-

Opposite: The interior of 'La Mezquita' at Jerez de la Frontera, Spain, a bodega belonging to the sherry and brandy producers Pedro Domecq SA. This remarkable structure was built in 1974 to the designs of Javier Soto for the storage of the rows of oak butts used in the maturation process of brandy. The repetition of columns and horseshoe arches was considered to be similar to that of the Great Mosque at Cordoba.

The mausoleum of King Mohammed V of Morocco at Rabat was built by his son Hassan II in the 1960s to the design of the Vietnamese architect Vo Toan. The full repertoire of traditional Moroccan arts and crafts were employed in this neo-Moorish building which adjoins the ruined twelfth-century Hassan Mosque.

able part of the city and the development incorporates a wide boulevard approaching the mosque complex, which includes a Koranic school, library and baths. King Hassan II commissioned its construction and design. The scale and dimensions of the mosque are vast, allegedly three times larger than the area of St Paul's Cathedral in London. The building consequently dominates the skyline of Casablanca. It is built over the Atlantic on a raft supported on reinforced concrete piles, alluding to a statement in the Koran which runs 'the throne of God was built on the water'. From the top of the minaret, 700 feet high and having a familiar, traditional Moorish profile, a laser beam shines in the direction of Mecca.

The decorative style of both interior and exterior are traditional but the hidden supporting structure depends on modern materials and the elaborately carved and painted timber ceiling over the central prayer space slides open mechanically in two huge sections. Apart from its sheer scale and the use of modern technology (both of which depart from Moorish tradition), the artificial lighting is by rows of giant Baroque-style multi-tiered chandeliers made from pale green Venetian crystal. These chandeliers are the only decorative items that have been imported. At the western end of the mosque there is a gallery for women, while at the eastern end there is a prayer chamber for the king. The architect is Marcel Pinseau, a Frenchman who also designed the royal palace at Agadir. Indeed, there is more than a hint of Versailles in the scale of the symmetrical layout of the boulevard and the mosque complex.

The difficulties in reconciling the beauty of traditional Islamic design with modern ideas of urban design and the large spaces needed for the circulation of the motorized traffic are demonstrated on the corniche at Jeddah, in Saudi Arabia. Here, and at other strategic positions in public areas of the city, many large-scale sculptures have been erected as a comprehensive beautification programme initiated by the former mayor, Sheikh Mohammed Said Farsi. They constitute what is probably the largest collection of recent modern open air sculpture anywhere in the public domain. The majority are unrelated to their Islamic context. There are several pieces by Henry Moore and other works by sculptors with an international reputation. None are figurative pieces, though some take Islamic themes. Several are large-scale three-dimensional renderings of Koranic quotations in Arabic calligraphy. One of these, in the overall form of a boat, was produced by Julio Lafuente, a Spanish architect, using computer-aided design techniques. A different theme was taken by Mustapha Senbel, who erected a sculpture entitled the *Ramadan*

Opposite: A view of the Great Mosque of Casablanca from the sea. King Hassan II commissioned the French architect Marcel Pinseau to design this vast structure which combines modern engineering technology with the large-scale use of traditional Moorish architectural and decorative elements. The siting on the ocean is said to relate to a quotation from the Koran which reads 'The throne of God was built on the water'.

Lantern on a small island. It is in the form of an enlarged traditional lantern and, when illuminated at night, its vivid colours are reflected in the sea. A similar motif on a larger scale is used in the *Mamlouk Mosque Lanterns*, another work by Julio Lafuente. Four lanterns in the Mamlouk tradition, enlarged to a great size and modelled from concrete and coloured glass, are suspended from a tubular steel framework. They too are best appreciated when illuminated at night. Perhaps the most interesting pieces in the sculpture collection are three works by the French-Hungarian Op Artist, Victor Vasarely, whose approach to visual art is based on abstract geometric shapes in plain colours arranged according to mathematical proportions. Two of them are three-dimensional renderings, in enamelled sheet steel, of the theme of the cube. They are reminiscent of Paul Klee's Bauhaus colour exercises in the tradition of Byzantine and Moorish mosaics.

As in the Great Mosque in Casablanca, modern technology has also been applied to a traditional theme in the design of the recent building for the Institute of the Arab World on a site overlooking the river Seine, in Paris. Its facilities include an auditorium and a library housing 35,000 volumes. The main facade is clad with 113 photo-sensitive hexagonal plates which, shaped like the diaphragm of a camera, move in order to control the flow of natural light and so maintain a constant intensity of light within. They are mounted in large square panels between two glass skins, the outer one of which is double-glazed. The intention is that they should be seen as a modern successor to the *mashrabiyya*. The building was designed by a French firm of architects, Nouvel, Lezènes and Soria, as the result of an international competition. In every other sense it is in the contemporary manner of the so-called 'high-tech' school with the hard expression of glass, stainless steel, white

Below: A sculpture on the corniche at Jeddah in the Kingdom of Saudi Arabia. It was created in the form of a boat by Julio Lafuente, a Spanish architect, and embodies a three-dimensional rendering of a calligraphic Koranic quotation. Computer-aided techniques were used in the shaping of the mould.

Another sculpture by Julio Lafuente seen at night on the corniche at Jeddah. It is named the Mamlouk Mosque Lanterns. Four giant lanterns made of concrete and coloured glass and suspended from a tubular steel framework appear dramatically against the night sky.

A night view of the entrance
facade of the Institute of
the Arab World in Paris.
The glass cladding is composed of a square grid
of panels incorporating
hexagonal photo-sensitive
plates. Except for the
geometric reference to
the Islamic tradition, the
building's design is typical
of the school of high technology. See also page 200.

marble and neutral grey tones. (It is no surprise to learn that the designer is an enthusiast for the genre of *film noir*.) The harsh industrialized environment thus created is in total contrast to the rich colourful quality of the exhibits on display within.

A different approach was taken by the designers of the Ismaili Centre, which was completed in 1983 on an island site opposite the Victoria and Albert Museum, in London. This was built to serve the religious, cultural and social needs of the Ismaili Muslim community. The brief to the designers, the Casson Conder Partnership, was for a building that would be sympathetic to the London context, not necessarily derived from Islamic precedents but in keeping with their mood. Without reverting to the obvious symbols of domes or Moorish arches, a kind of trabeated architecture, combined with the subtle use of geometry in the shaping of form and surface, succeeds in suggesting an Islamic character. Externally, line and proportion have been expressed in the relation between the materials; granite, glass, hardwood and textured concrete. The interior makes a more direct reference to the Islamic geometric tradition. A Muslim, Karl Schlamminger, who designed the finishes of the main entrance and the Prayer Hall at second-floor level, was also responsible for the ceiling patterns that provide a thematic link for the rest of the building, including the social spaces at first-floor level, as well as for the design of the geometric patterning of the carpets and curtains. The predominant colour of the interior is white with line and pattern rendered in blues, greens and neutral tones. Handrails are in stainless steel, in keeping with the designer's aim to achieve a cool and serene atmosphere. In the Prayer Hall a richer effect is achieved by the use of a variety of marbles on the walls, perforated grilles at the windows and teak frames with Kufic calligraphy. Further reference to Moorish tradition is made in the layout of the roof level of this four-storey building. Here an enclosed patio garden has been symmetrically divided into quarters with a central fountain on an eight-starred plan. The surrounding committee and reading rooms have windows with direct views into the garden.

In these contemporary buildings in Paris and London, linear pattern and proportion are the means of making visual reference to Moorish tradition. Rich colours and elaborate carving are omitted from the design and detailing. This more puritanical approach may be due to the influence of the Modern Movement in the West, which is still powerful, in spite of the acceptance of sometimes banal and eclectic references to historic styles in the so-called Post-Modern style. Integrated ornament and polychrome decorative effects are rare externally or internally in the contemporary buildings of Western countries. Uninhibited colours and shapes are confined to works of art in galleries and prosperous homes where the emphasis is often on mobility, value and re-sale. In the Islamic world, however, popular desire for luxuriant colour and pattern as an integral part of architecture, both externally and internally, continues to be strong.

This popular taste for ornament is vividly demonstrated in a complex of buildings completed in the village of Bhong, midway between Karachi and Lahore, in Pakistan. This group, centred around a mosque, was built over a period of fifty years, between 1932 and 1982. Its development over such a long period was due to the leadership of one person, Rais Ghazi Mohammed, who wanted to create a congregational mosque, a centre of learning and a source of employment for people involved in building and the decorative crafts who were attracted to Bhong from many parts of Pakistan and India. The full range of traditional materi-

als was obtained from various centres in Pakistan, except for limited amounts of black marble which were imported from Europe. As in the recent Moroccan mosques, modern materials were used mainly for structural purposes (even though synthetic materials, such as plastic tiles; terrazzo and coloured cement occur in some of the ancillary buildings). The mosque interiors were decorated solely with traditional materials. The stylistic elements were derived from historic monuments throughout the geographical area that produced the Moorish style: Mogul India, Persia, Turkey, Spain and Morocco. There are also colonial influences in the design of the palace adjoining the mosque and the *madrassa*. In 1986 the complex received an Aga Khan Award for Architecture; in their accompanying statement, members of the jury expressed their wish to acknowledge the diversity that enriches popular taste, going on to observe that its use and misuse of traditional signs and symbols expressed the growing pains of an architecture in transition. The vitality of the total effect of the indiscriminate mixture of elements is, as Serageldin comments, reminiscent of the heedless vulgarity of some nineteenth-century American millionaires. The beauty of individual elements and the breathtaking dexterity of the craftsmen are obvious but a rigorous overall design concept is lacking.

There is little doubt that Moorish style — embodied in the decorative skills of stuccowork, joincry, ceramics and the setting-out and painting of geometric and arabesque patterns — is alive in Islamic countries from Pakistan to Morocco, and that it survives for reasons of religious conviction, aesthetic conservatism and some degree of popular demand. This is particularly true in Morocco, whose native craftsmen are in great demand by the richer nations for work on new mosques and other religious buildings. The appeal of Moorish style for the wealthy in Western countries, however, is now limited to mobile art objects seen to combine investment potential with aesthetic quality. The ease of international air travel has irreversibly altered the West's perception of exotic cultures. The decline of the cinema has also removed a context in which exoticism could be artificially created. There thus remains no demand from Westerners at any income level for Moorish style in the buildings they inhabit or frequent. The only exception is the provision of buildings related to the religious and cultural needs of Islamic minority communities. These usually embody the style in a fairly restrained manner, at least externally. Moorish style has always been in transition, in a state of evolution, and this is as true today as at

Opposite: Part of the ground floor elevation of the Ismaili Centre on a site opposite the Victoria and Albert Museum. It was designed by the Casson Conder Partnership and completed in 1983. The trabeated nature of the structure is expressed in rectangular line and proportion with an emphasis on the vertical. There is fine timber latticework to the ground-floor windows and the exterior colour scheme relies on natural finishes.

The inner entrance hall of the Ismaili Centre in London, showing the predominantly white interior with the geometric patterns of the octagonal skylight over the stairs to the Prayer Hall lined in cool colours and neutral tones.

any time in its history. It is only the rate of change that varies; at times it has been so slow as to appear non-existent. At present, speed is increasing, while technology and Western cultural influence continue to provide new challenges. As we have seen, intellectuals and professional designers have tended to shy away from the style's vigorous use of colour and pattern. A few, like Issam El-Said, have shown that it is possible to extend the tradition in a vital manner that does not directly imitate the past, especially in the field of calligra-phy. A style that embodies the essential discipline of geometry and the repeat pattern is certain to be seen as a style in which the computer has a role. Critchlow and Marchant have been able to show how intricate Islamic repeat patterns based on the *zillij* can be generated in line and colour by computer. This initial step was used to aid the design process. Whether it will be extended to setting-out and production remains a matter of speculation. If this does happen, the implications could be far-reaching.

GLOSSARY

Abbasid The Sunni dynasty which controlled much of the Islamic world from Baghdad between AD 749 and 1258.

Almohad The Berber dynasty which ucceeded the Almoravids in North Africa and Spain. An ascetic group, they dominated the area from AD 1130 to 1269.

Almoravid The ascetic Berber dynasty which created an empire in North Africa and Spain. Their influence lasted from AD 1056 to 1147.

Alcazar (Spanish, from Arabic) A fortified house or palace.

Al Andalus (from Arabic) Islamic Spain.

Aquamanile (Latin) A vessel used to hold and pour water.

Arabesque (from French) A stylized and intertwined plant motif developed from the spiralling vine with leaves and tendrils.

Artesonado (Spanish) A style of Spanish joinery with Islamic precedent. The term is usually applied to coffered ceilings.

Ayn (Arabic) A fountain.

Azulejo (Spanish) A glazed tile.

Bejmat (Arabic) Rectangular ceramic floor tiles made in the Moroccan tradition.

Buteh (Persian) Meaning shrub, the buteh is the teardrop shape on which the paisley pattern is based.

Caliph (Arabic) The title adopted by the successors of Mohammed, as supreme heads of the Muslim community.

Cantiga (Spanish) A medieval narrative poem set to music.

Celosia (Spanish) A perforated stone screen.

Chahar bagh (Persian) A garden divided into quadrants by water channels symbolizing the four rivers of Paradise.

Convivencia (Spanish) The co-existence of the people of the three religions in medieval Spain.

Coptic Relating to the ancient Christian church of Egypt.

Costumbrismo (Spanish) The style of literature which gives particular emphasis to the local manners and customs of a specific region. Important in the literature of nineteenth-century Spain.

Cuenca (Spanish) Bowl/hollow. A technique used for decorating ceramic tiles in which the pattern is formed as hollows in the surface of the tile, leaving a raised outline to keep different glaze colours separate.

Cuerda seca (Spanish) Dry cord. A technique used for decorating ceramic tiles in which a cord (or a mixture of manganese and grease) burned away during firing separates the glazes and leaves a slight depression between the colours.

Damascene A technique used to decorate steel by etching, encrusting or inlaying to produce a watered appearance.

Diwan (from Persian) Originally account books or a collection of poems, diwan has come to mean a reception room and thence the ruler and his council or a government office.

Diwan-i-Am (from Persian) A public audience hall.

Diwan-i-Khas (from Persian) A private udience hall.

Durbar (from Persian) An imperial reception. Originally Mogul, but later adopted by the British in India.

Farsi The Persian style of Arabic script. (Also the language of modern Iran.) The thickness of the line varies, creating contrast and curvature.

Fatimid The dynasty of the Shi'a sect which established itself in North Africa and expanded into Egypt and Syria. It lasted from AD 909 to 1171.

Frit (from Latin) A mixture of refined clay and ground quartz which, when fired, becomes vitrified.

Hadith The tradition recording the words of Mohammed and his Companions. Second only to the Koran in importance.

Hammam (Arabic) A bathhouse.

Harem (from Arabic) The private family quarters of a Muslim house.

Imam (Arabic) The prayer leader in a mosque. Also applied to the leader of the entire Islamic community.

Jali (Urdu) A perforated stone screen in Mogul India.

Jami' (Arabic) A term applied to an important mosque in which the Friday noon prayer is led from the minbar.

Juderia The Jewish quarter of a medieval Spanish town.

Keel arch (also known as ogee arch) A pointed arch with an S-shaped curve on either side.

Khan (Turkish) A prince or governor.

Kiosk (Turkish) A pavilion for entertainment.

Koran The holy scripture of Islam, containing the revelation of the Prophet Mohammed.

Kufic An early Arabic script which is thick, compressed and angular and often discontinuous.

Kulliye (Turkish) A complex consisting of a mosque, several madrassas, a hospital, a hostel and a soup kitchen.

Madrassa (Arabic) A Muslim school, particularly a theological college.

Maghreb (Arabic) That part of north-west Africa which stretches from Morocco to Libya.

Mahal (Urdu) A palace in Mogul India.

Mamlouk (Arabic) Literally a slave of non-Islamic origin but applied to the dynasty that became the ruling class of Egypt from 1250 to 1517.

Marinids The dynasty that succeeded the Almohads and ruled Morocco from AD 1196 to 1549.

Mashrabiyya (Arabic) Latticework of turned or carved wood used for screens or enclosing balconies where privacy and ventilation are needed.

Masjid (Arabic) Literally a place of prostration and thus a mosque.

Meidan (Persian) A public open square or plaza.

Merlon A projection between the embrasures of the battlements of a parapet wall.

Mezquita (Spanish) A mosque.

Mihrab (from Arabic) A niche in the mosque wall indicating the direction of Mecca.

Minbar (from Arabic) A pulpit or flight of steps set to the right of the mihrab for the reading of the Friday sermon in a mosque.

Minaret A tower, usually part of or closely adjoining a mosque, from which the muezzin makes his call to prayer.

Mogul (Persian) The dynasty originating from Mongolia which conquered and ruled India in the sixteenth century.

Moresque (from French) A term used from the sixteenth to the nineteenth centuries (by Owen Jones, among others) to mean Moorish.

Morisco (Spanish) A Muslim who converted to Christianity at the time of the Reconquest in Spain.

Mozarab (from Arabic) Relating to the Christians who lived in Islamic Spain.

Mudéjar (Spanish) Relating to the Muslims who remained in Christian Spain and to the style of architecture that largely derived from their culture.

Muezzin (from Arabic) The mosque official who makes the public call to prayer.

Muqarna (Arabic) A niche forming part of a decorative honeycomb, often compared with stalactites and used for internal treatment of curved surfaces and especially in the transitional zones between domes and their supports.

Nameh (Persian) A body of writing.

Naskhi The standard Arabic cursive script.

Nasrid The dynasty centred on Granada which ruled Andalusia from AD 1246 to 1492.

Odalisque (from French/Turkish) A female slave or concubine.

Orientalist Relating to the school of European artists in the nineteenth and early twentieth centuries who painted exotic themes from the East, including North Africa but usually excluding China and Japan.

Ottoman (from French) Relating to the Turkish dynasty, founded by Othman in the thirteenth century, which conquered the Near East and invaded Europe in the sixteenth century. The Ottoman sultanate was finally abolished in 1922. Also used to refer to a long low upholstered sofa.

Qibla (Arabic) The direction of Mecca which Muslims must face when praying.

Rejola (Spanish) The standard brick, theoretically two hands by one in size, which was used by the Mudéjar builders of Aragon.

Rowshan (Arabic) A timber latticed balcony window, similar to a mashrabiyya.

Sahn (Arabic) The central courtyard in front of a mosque.

Safavid The dynasty which ruled Persia from AD 1501 to 1722. They made Isfahan their capital.

Saracenic Relating to Muslims, usually of Arab origin, especially opponents of the Crusaders. General term of Latin origin used, especially in the nineteenth century, for Islamic architecture but now obsolete.

Sarai (Turkish) A palace.

Seljuk The dynasty from Central Asia that ruled Persia and Iraq from AD 1038 to 1194.

Shari'a (Arabic) Literally the road. Has now come to mean the body of Islamic law regulating religious and secular duties and prohibitions.

Shemassiat (Arabic) Windows of coloured glass set in carved gypsum frames.

Shi'a Relating to the sect of Islam which believes in a hereditary caliphate descending from Ali, the son-in-law of Mohammed.

Squinch A section of a vault which acts as an intermediary between a square or rectangular room and the circular dome above.

Stucco (from Italian) A gypsum plaster used for coating walls and making decorative casts.

Sufi A Muslim mystic.

Sunni Relating to the major sect of Islam (the other being the Shi'a), which rejects the theory of a hereditary caliphate.

Sura Any of the 114 chapters of the Koran.

Taifa (Arabic) A petty dynasty. Islamic Spain was ruled by a number of these after the fall of the Umayyads.

Talmud (Hebrew) The code of Jewish civil and canon law.

Thuluth A cursive Arabic script with a bounding rhythm. A development of Naskhi, it is often used for large inscriptions.

Torah (Hebrew) Strictly speaking, the Pentateuch or first five books of the Old Testament, but it has come to mean the whole body of Jewish law.

Trabeated Constructed with horizontal beams, as opposed to arches or vaults.

Tugra (Turkish) The stylized calligraphic monogram of a Turkish sultan.

Umayyad The dynasty which ruled the Muslim world from Damascus from AD 661 to 750 when they were overthrown by the Abbasids. A branch of the Umayyads established itself in Spain between AD 756 and 1031.

Visigoths The Western Goths who emigrated to southern France and Spain and established a Christian kingdom there prior to the Muslim invasion in the eighth century.

Voussoir A wedge-shaped stone that is used with others to create an arch.

Waqf (Arabic) An endowed foundation or trust which supports mosques, madrassas and other public buildings in a Muslim community.

Zillij (Arabic) Glazed ceramic tiles cut in geometric forms.

PLACES TO VISIT

There follows a selected list of buildings of interest and places to visit. It is not in any sense comprehensive. Access to the interior prayer spaces of mosques is not normally possible for non-Muslims.

CHAPTERS 1–5

Agra, India
Taj Mahal
The most famous Mogul shrine, set in a magnificent garden on the banks of the river Jumna.

Red Fort
A sixteenth-century Mogul fort, incorporating a magnificent palace and reception halls.

Ahmadabad, India
Mosque of Sidi Sayyid
A fifteenth-century mosque containing the exquisite 'Tree of Life' grille window in carved stone.

Baghdad, Iraq
Palace in the Qala
A palace built in brickwork during the early thirteenth century on a courtyard plan.

Bukhara, Uzbekistan
Tomb of Ismail Samani
A square domed tomb built in patterned brickwork during the tenth century.

Cairo, Egypt
Ibn Tulun Mosque
A noble brick mosque faced in stucco and built in the ninth century.

Qaitbay Mosque
A fifteenth-century Mamlouk complex including a tomb and madrassa.

Sultan Hassan Mosque
A large-scale fourteenth-century complex incorporating a madrassa and the tomb of Mamlouk Sultan Hassan.

House of Gamal El Din Al Dhahabi
A typical Ottoman merchant's house dating from the seventeenth century. Currently the headquarters of the Committee for the Preservation of Arab Monuments.

Cordoba, Spain
Great Mosque
A former mosque with a beautiful interior, which was built in the eighth century and extended over the following two centuries.

Damascus, Syria
Great Mosque
A large mosque dating from the eighth century and containing important mosaics.

Edirne, Turkey
Selimiye Mosque
A splendid sixteenth-century Ottoman mosque complex, considered by many to be the finest work of Sinan.

Fatehpur Sikri, India
A magnificent city, capital of the Mogul emperor Akbar, containing many red sandstone structures that display the influence and skills of Hindu masons.

Fez, Morocco
Bou Inania Mosque
A fourteenth-century mosque and madrassa with a large courtyard, prayer hall and minaret.

Granada, Spain
Alhambra and Generalife
The legendary fourteenth-century fortified palace and gardens that display the complete repertoire of Moorish style.

Isfahan, Iran
Mosque of Lutfullah
The polychrome ceramics of the entrance portal and dome of this seventeenth-century mosque are prominent from the Meidan.

Shah's Mosque
The large polychrome entrance, portal, minarets and elegantly decorated dome are also visible from the Meidan.

Ali Kapu
The main gate and reception pavilion to the Safavid royal palace. The interior is sumptuous.

Chehel Situn
The garden pavilion of the royal palace with a portico of twenty columns.

Istanbul, Turkey
Hagia Sophia
A celebrated and monumental domed Byzantine church of the sixth century. It was converted to a mosque in the Ottoman era and is now a museum.

Suleimaniye Mosque
An impressive Ottoman mosque complex designed by Sinan in the sixteenth century.

Topkapi Palace
The Ottoman imperial palace and seat of government arranged around three courtyards. It contains an extensive collection of works of art.

Jeddah, Saudi Arabia
Old Quarter
Restored traditional houses with projecting timber balconies in the Red Sea style.

Jerusalem, Israel
Dome of the Rock
The sacred Muslim structure built at the end of the seventh century over the rock whence the Prophet Mohammed ascended to heaven.

Lahore, Pakistan
Shalamar Garden
A formal water gardens and a royal pavilion laid out for the Mogul emperor, Shah Jehan, in the seventeenth century.

Marrakesh, Morocco
Koutoubia Mosque
A twelfth-century mosque of the Almohad dynasty with an imposing minaret by the architect who designed the structure of La Giralda at Seville.

Meknes, Morocco
Bou Inania Madrassa
A fourteenth-century madrassa, similar to, but smaller than, the one at Fez.

Quintinilla de las Viñas, Spain
Nuestra Señora de las Viñas (near Burgos)
A small Visigothic church of the seventh century with beautiful stone friezes on the outside walls and horseshoe arch openings to the sanctuary.

Qusair Amra, Jordan
A solitary Umayyad hunting lodge of the eighth century containing a bathhouse and painted murals.

Rabat, Morocco
Gate of Chella
A decorative gateway with a pointed arch built in the fourteenth century to give access to the necropolis of Chella.

Saragossa, Spain
Aljaferia
A fortified Muslim palace of the eleventh century containing a small mosque, a later Mudéjar courtyard and a throne room for Ferdinand and Isabella.

Seville, Spain
Alcazar
A magnificent palace rebuilt for the Christian King Pedro by Moorish craftsmen in the fourteenth century.

La Giralda
The twelfth-century minaret to the demolished Great Mosque with the Christian addition of a lantern for the bells and a revolving statue.

Sikandra, India
Akbar's Mausoleum (near Agra)
The early seventeenth-century tomb of the great Mogul emperor with four white minarets and decorative portals.

Teruel, Spain
Cathedral
A brick cathedral with a Mudéjar bell tower and a decorative timber ceiling.

San Salvador
A church with a spectacular bell tower with Mudéjar brick and ceramic decoration.

Testour, Tunisia
Friday Mosque
A seventeenth-century brick mosque with a minaret in Mudéjar decorative style.

Toledo, Spain
Cristo de la Luz
A former brick mosque dating from the end of the tenth century which has been converted into a church with Mudéjar additions.

El Tránsito
A fourteenth-century synagogue with intricate decoration and calligraphy. A museum of Sephardic culture adjoins the synagogue.

Santa Maria la Blanca
A former synagogue of the thirteenth century, later converted to a church.

Tozeur, Tunisia
Friday Mosque
A brick mosque in Mudéjar style with a minaret similar to that at Testour.

CHAPTER 6

Barcelona, Spain
Casa Vicens
A private house designed by Antoni Gaudí in 1883 with a colourful exterior in an individual version of Mudéjar style.

Guell Park
A park containing several remarkable structures by Gaudí, including a museum and a unique continuous curved bench faced with polychromatic ceramics.

Berlin, Germany
Oranienburgerstrasse Synagogue
A synagogue built with elaborate Moorish elements to the designs of Edward Knoblauch in the 1860s.

Brighton, UK
Royal Pavilion
A seaside residence designed by John Nash and built in 1815 for the Prince Regent. Only the exterior and gardens are Moorish in style.

Budapest, Hungary
Dohany utca Synagogue
A very large synagogue in the Moorish style designed by Forster in the 1850s. It now incorporates a Jewish museum.

Cardiff, UK
Cardiff Castle
A huge Neo-Gothic pile containing an opulent Arab room designed by William Burges in 1880.

Dunfermline, UK
Carnegie Centre
A classical revival building dating from 1905 and containing a Turkish suite in Moorish style with colourful ceramics.

Edinburgh, UK
Drumsheugh Baths
A private club with a swimming bath designed in Moorish style in 1882.

Florence, Italy
Via Farmi Synagogue
A prominent synagogue in Moorish style, completed in 1882.

Greendale, New York State, USA
Olana
The studio house built by the painter Frederick Church to house his collection of Islamic objets d'art.

Lima, Peru
Palacio de Torre Tagle
An eighteenth-century palace with timber balconies in the Moorish tradition. Now the Peruvian Foreign Ministry.

Archbishop's Palace
Built in the 1940s and following the Torre Tagle tradition with projecting timber balconies.

Liverpool, UK
Princes Road Synagogue
A synagogue with an elaborate Moorish Revival interior designed by W and G Audsley in 1874.

London, UK
Leighton House
The studio house of the painter Lord Leighton with an extension known as the Arab Hall.

Madras, India
University Senate House
Built in 1879 in what was then called the Indo-Saracenic style to the designs of Robert Chisholm.

Law Courts
A vast complex designed in the Indo-Saracenic style by Henry Irwin and completed in 1892.

Mexico City, Mexico
La Casa de los Azulejos
A large mansion built in 1596 with an extensive use of coloured ceramics, hence its name. It is now Sanborn's restaurant.

Moreton-in-Marsh, UK
Sezincote
A country house completed in 1810 for Sir Charles Cockerell. The exterior and gardens are in a romantic version of the Mogul style.

Mysore, India
Maharajah's Palace
A huge palace designed at the beginning of the twentieth century by Henry Irwin in a hybrid style. It contains a durbar hall with Mogul elements and exotic stained glass.

Natchez, Mississippi, USA
Longwood
An unusual octagonal house built in Moorish style to the design of Samuel Sloan for a cotton planter in the 1850s.

Puebla, Mexico
Casa del Alfeñique
A mansion faced with glazed and unglazed ceramics in Mudéjar manner. Now a museum.

Cathedral
A seventeenth-century cathedral with a dome faced with coloured ceramic tiles in Mudéjar tradition.

Quito, Ecuador
San Francisco
A church with a painted timber ceiling in Mudéjar style.

Rignano dell'Arno, Italy
Villa de Sanmezzanno
A large villa near Florence with a spectacular Moorish interior. It belonged to the Marchese Panciatichi who transformed it during the 1850s.

Santiago, Chile
Palacio La Alhambra
A large mansion built around two courtyards in the style of the Alhambra. Now a cultural centre.

CHAPTER 7

Barcelona, Spain
Plaza de Toros Monumental
A large bull ring completed in 1915 in a mixture of Mudéjar and Secession styles.

Casablanca, Morocco
Great Mosque of Hassan II
A huge mosque built in Moorish style on piles over the sea. Completed in 1993.

Jeddah, Saudi Arabia
Corniche
A public space along the seafront where there are many modern sculptures showing Moorish and Islamic influences.

Jerez de la Frontera, Spain
'La Mezquita'
A large bodega used for the maturation of brandy by Pedro Domecq SA. It has an impressive interior in Moorish style and was built in 1974.

Kansas City, USA
Country Club Plaza
A shopping precinct containing many buildings in Moorish style including the Giralda tower. Dating from the period between the 1920s and 1950s.

London, UK
Astoria Cinema
A cinema in Finsbury Park built in the 1930s in a blend of Moorish and Byzantine styles. The Fountain Court is particularly notable.

Ismaili Centre
A religious centre opposite the Victoria and Albert Museum. Completed in 1983 in a contemporary version of Islamic style.

Opa Locka, USA
City Hall
The most extravagant building in a northern suburb of Miami. Built in the 1920s in a predominantly neo-Moorish style.

Paris, France
Institute of the Arab World
A multi-storey building in the modern 'high tech' style, except for the Moorish patterning of the glass window walls.

Rabat, Morocco
Tomb of Mohammed V
Erected in the 1960s in a neo-Moorish style using the full repertoire of Moorish crafts. It is situated close to the twelfth-century minaret of Hassan.

Rochefort, France
Loti Museum
The former house of Pierre Loti, decorated in Moorish style and containing the writer's collection of memorabilia.

Saragossa, Spain
Central Market
A market building with details in iron, brick and stone deriving from Mudéjar precedent. Dates from the turn of the century.

Kiosko de la Musica
A bandstand dating from the Spanish-French Exhibition of 1908. A lively design showing Mudéjar influence.

Post Office
A prominent public building built in 1917 with a brick facade with stone dressing. It also shows strong Mudéjar influence.

Seville, Spain
Museo de Artes y Costumbres
A museum which was originally the Mudéjar Pavilion of the 1929 Spanish-American Exhibition.

BIBLIOGRAPHY

Akbar, A. *Discovering Islam.* London: Routledge, 1988.

Al-Kardabus, Ibn. *Historia de Al-Andalus.* Madrid: Akal, 1986.

Al-Sayyad, N, ed. *Forms of Dominance.* Aldershot: Avebury, 1992.

Albarn, K, & others. *The Language of Pattern.* London: Thames & Hudson, 1974.

Archer, M, & Lightbown, R. *India Observed.* London: Victoria & Albert Museum, 1982.

Arts Council of Great Britain. *The Arts of Islam.* London: 1976. Exhibition catalogue.

Arts Council of Great Britain. *Homage to Barcelona.* London: 1986. Exhibition catalogue.

Atwell, D. *Cathedrals of the Movies.* London: Architectural Press, 1980.

Bakhtiar, L. *Sufi.* London: Thames & Hudson, 1976.

Baroda, M. *The Palaces of India.* London: HarperCollins, 1980.

Barrucand, M, & Bednorz, A. *Moorish Architecture in Andalusia.* Cologne: Taschen, 1992.

Breffny, B de. *The Synagogue.* London: Weidenfeld & Nicolson, 1978.

Brend, B. *Islamic Art.* London: British Museum Press, 1991.

Burckhardt, T. *Moorish Culture in Spain.* London: Allen & Unwin, 1972.

Burckhardt, T. *Art of Islam.* London: World of Islam, 1976.

Calvert, A F. *Moorish Remains in Spain.* London: Lane, 1906.

Cant, M. *Villages of Edinburgh.* Edinburgh: Donald, 1986.

Castedo, L. *A History of Latin American Art & Architecture.* London: Pall Mall, 1969.

Conner, P. *Oriental Architecture of the West.* London: Thames & Hudson, 1979.

Crespi, G. *Gli Arabi in Europa.* Milan: Jaca, 1979.

Cresti, C. *Civiltà delle Ville Toscane.* Udine: Magnus, 1992.

Creswell, K A C. *Early Muslim Architecture.* Harmondsworth: Penguin, 1958.

Critchlow, K. *Islamic Patterns.* New York: Schocken, 1976.

Crowe, S & Haywood, S. *The Gardens of Mughul India.* London: Thames & Hudson, 1972.

Danby, M. *The Fires of Excellence: Spanish and Portuguese Oriental Architecture.* Reading: Garnet, 1997.

Darby, M. *The Islamic Perspective.* London: World of Islam, 1983.

Dore, H. *William Morris.* London: Pyramid, 1990.

Dunn, R E. *Adventures of Ibn Battuta.* London: Croom Helm, 1986.

El-Said, I. *Islamic Art & Architecture: The System of Geometric Design.* Reading: Garnet, 1993.

El-Said, I, & Parman, A. *Geometric Concepts in Islamic Art.* London: World of Islam, 1976.

Ettinghausen, R & Grabar, O. *The Art and Architecture of Islam 650–1250.* Harmondsworth: Penguin, Pelican History of Art, 1987.

Farsi, H M S. *Jeddah: City of Art.* London: Stacey, 1991.

Ferrier, R W, ed. *The Arts of Persia.* New Haven: Yale University Press, 1989.

Fletcher, R. *Moorish Spain.* London: Weidenfeld & Nicolson, 1992.

Fraser, V. *The Architecture of Conquest.* Cambridge: Cambridge University Press, 1990.

Garner, P. *Twentieth-Century Furniture.* Oxford: Phaidon Press, 1980.

Ghulam, Y M. *The Art of Arabic Calligraphy.* Riyadh: Department of Antiquities, 1982.

Gibb, H A R (trans). *Travels of Ibn Battuta.* Cambridge: Cambridge University Press, 1958-62.

Glasstone, V. *Victorian & Edwardian Theatres.* London: Thames & Hudson, 1975.

Gobierno de Aragón. *Signos-Arte y Cultura en el Alto Aragón.* Huesca: 1993. Exhibition catalogue.

Goitia, F C. *Historia de la Arquitectura Española-Edad Antigua y Edad Media.* Madrid: 1965.

Goitia, F C. *The Mosque of Cordoba.* Granada: Albaicin, 1971.

Gomez, E G, & Pareja, J B. *L'Alhambra: le Palais Royal.* Granada: Albaicin, 1969.

Goodwin, G. *Islamic Architecture: Ottoman Turkey.* London: Scorpion, 1977.

Goodwin, G. *Islamic Spain.* Harmondsworth: Penguin, 1991.

Grabar, O. *The Formation of Islamic Art.* New Haven: Yale University Press, 1973.

Greenlaw, J P. *The Coral Buildings of Suakin.* Stocksfield: Oriel, 1976.

Gualis, G M B, Guatas, M G, & Lasaosa, J G. *Zaragoza a Principios del S. XX: El Modernismo.* Saragossa: General, 1977.

Gualis, G M B. *Arte Mudéjar Aragonés.* Saragossa: Guara, 1978.

Gualis, G M B. *El Arte Mudéjar.* Teruel: Instituto de Estudios Turolenses, 1990.

Hambly, G. *Cities of Mughul India.* London: Paul Elek, 1977.

Hansen, H J. *Late Nineteenth Century Art.* Newton Abbot: David & Charles, 1973.

Harvey, L P. *Islamic Spain 1250 to 1500.* Chicago: Chicago University Press, 1992.

Hedgecoe, J, & Damluji, S S. *Zillij: The Art of Moroccan Ceramics.* Reading: Garnet, 1992.

Hill, D, & Golvin, G. *Islamic Architecture in North Africa.* London: Faber & Faber, 1976.

Hoag, J D. *Islamic Architecture.* London: Faber & Faber, 1987.

Hutt, A. *Islamic Architecture: North Africa.* London: Scorpion, 1977.

Hutt, A & Harrow, L. *Islamic Architecture: Iran 1.* London: Scorpion, 1977.

Jean, G. *Writing: The Story of Alphabets and Scripts.* London: Thames & Hudson, 1992.

Jones, O. *The Grammar of Ornament.* London: Studio Editions, 1986.

Jullian, P. *The Orientalists.* Oxford: Phaidon Press, 1977.

Khaldoun, Ibn. *The Muqaddimah.* New York: Pantheon, 1958.

Lafuente, J L C & Gonzalvo, F J P, eds. *La Cultura Islámica En Aragón.* Saragossa: Diputación Provincial, 1986.

Lane, E W. *Manners and Customs of the Modern Egyptians.* London: East-West, 1978.

Levey, M. *The World of Ottoman Art.* London: Thames & Hudson, 1975.

Lindemann, G. *History of German Art.* London: Pall Mall, 1971.

Loukomski, G. *Jewish Art in European Synagogues.* London: Hutchinson, 1947.

Mackay, A. *Spain in the Middle Ages.* London: Macmillan, 1977.

Marçais, G. *L'Architecture Musulmane d'Occident.* Paris: 1955.

Metcalf, T R. *An Imperial Vision.* London: Faber & Faber, 1989.

Moneo, R. *The Life of Buildings: The Cordoba Mosque Extensions.* Lausanne: Ecole Polytechnique, 1983.

Montgomery Watt. *The Majesty that was Islam.* London: Sidgwick & Jackson, 1974.

Murphy, J C. *The Arabian Antiquities of Spain.* Granada: Procyta, 1987.

Nasr, S H. *Islamic Science.* London: World of Islam, 1976.

Newark, T. *Emile Gallé.* Secaucus, New Jersey: Chartwell, 1989.

Ordax, S A & Alvarez, J A. *La Ermita de Santa Maria-Quintinilla de Las Viñas.* Burgos: C. D. Ahorros Municipal, 1982.

Paccard, A. *Traditional Islamic Craft in Moroccan Architecture.* Saint-Jorioz: Atelier 74, 1980.

Palol, P D. *Arte Hispanico de la Epoca Visigoda.* Barcelona: Poligrafa, 1968.

Read, J. *The Moors in Spain & Portugal.* London: Faber & Faber, 1974.

Reilly, V. *Paisley Patterns.* London: Studio Editions, 1989.

Rewald, S. *Paul Klee.* London: Tate Gallery, 1989. Catalogue.

Rivoira, G T. *Moslem Architecture.* Oxford: Oxford University Press, 1918.

Rogers, M. *The Spread of Islam.* Oxford: Phaidon Press, 1976.

Said, E W. *Orientalism.* London: Penguin, 1985.

Sanford, T E. *The Story of Architecture in Mexico.* New York: Norton, 1947.

Schuyler, M. *American Architecture and Other Writings.* Harvard: Harvard University Press, 1961.

Sebastian, M E, Gracia, J L P, & Sauras, M I S. *La Aljaferia de Zaragoza.* Saragossa: Cortes de Aragón, 1986.

Serageldin, I. *Space for Freedom.* London: Butterworth, 1986.

Stevens, M A, ed. *The Orientalists: Delacroix to Matisse.* London: Royal Academy, 1984.

Stewart, D. *The Alhambra.* London: Reader's Digest, 1974.

Sweetman, J. *The Oriental Obsession.* Cambridge: Cambridge University Press, 1988.

Talbot Rice, D. *Islamic Art.* London: Thames & Hudson, 1965.

Topsfield, A. *An Introduction to Indian Court Painting.* London: H. M. Stationery Office, 1984.

Trevelyan, R. *Shades of the Alhambra.* London: Secker & Warburg, 1985.

Tzonis, & Lefaivre. *Architecture in Europe since 1968.* London: Thames & Hudson, 1992.

Veron, J M. *Arquitectura Aragonesa: 1885-1920.* Saragossa: C. O. de Arquitectos de Aragón, 1993.

Viguera, M J. *Aragón Musulman.* Saragossa: General, 1981.

Wilson, E. *Islamic Designs.* London: British Museum Press, 1988.

Zamora, M I A. *Ceramica Aragonesa.* Saragossa: General, 1982.

Zerbst, R. *Antoni Gaudí.* Cologne: Taschen, 1988.

INDEX

Page numbers in italic refer to the illustrations and captions

ACKNOWLEDGEMENTS

I am indebted to the team at Phaidon for their help and dedication.

Amongst the many people who have helped me at different stages in the collection of background information, I would like to express my gratitude to Sundus Omer Ali, Mohammed Hayder Asaad, Jaime Buesa, Carlos Buil, Neville Conder, Beltrán Domecq, Sheikh Mohammed Farsi, José Granádos, Jean Pierre Greenlaw, Edwin Haramoto, Manuel Herz, David Hicks, Saj Jivanjee, John Lindsay, Hernan Montecinos, Professor Magdy Nour, Isaam El Said and Dr Esmat El Said.

I would like to thank my wife Ilse for her assistance and encouragement and my daughters Josephine and Claudia for their enthusiastic interest.

PICTURE CREDITS